Trump
Trust the Plan

Why Donald Trump Needs to Win 2020

Also, by Clark Prasad

Baramulla Bomber
Mirror Mirror, (The Gollancz Book of South Asian Science Fiction)

DEDICATION

To COVID Warriors
To Humanity
To Our Children
To Undiscovered Ideas
& To the idea of Q

A Prayer

The Armor of God

Finally, be strong in the Lord and in his mighty power. Put on the full armor of God so that you can take your stand against the devil's schemes. For our struggle is not against flesh and blood, but against the rulers, against the authorities, against the powers of this dark world and against the spiritual forces of evil in the heavenly realms. Therefore, put on the full armor of God, so that when the day of evil comes, you may be able to stand your ground, and after you have done everything, to stand. Stand firm then, with the belt of truth buckled around your waist, with the breastplate of righteousness in place, and with your feet fitted with the readiness that comes from the gospel of peace. In addition to all this, take up the shield of faith, with which you can extinguish all the flaming arrows of the evil one. 17 Take the helmet of salvation and the sword of the Spirit, which is the word of God.

And pray in the Spirit on all occasions with all kinds of prayers and requests. With this in mind, be alert and always keep on praying for all the Lord's people.

Have faith in Humanity. | Have faith in Yourself. | Have faith in God.

The Great Awakening.

A Note

I have written this book in under a month, but the story, thoughts, and writing have been built over two decades. My relationship with the USA began with me visiting USA as a kid in 1984 for a month. A week in Florida, and Disneyland was my highlight. Later, with my visits to American Center Library in Delhi, India. There I read about the Founding Fathers, the history, listened to different views, and kept following the stories. For me USA was about Freedom, Liberty, and Free Thought. Where one can rise on their own merit and not be pulled down by systemic forces. And many Indians have succeeded. So, have so many other cultures and individuals.

Over the years, I saw USA change, and in this period of Sept-Oct 2020, I felt the need to write this book. I wanted to share some thoughts (it is allowed now, who knows if it will be the same in the future). Please do bear with me if there are specific gaps in language or some points. I have tied to provide sources wherever I could. My aim here is to write why Trump needs to win the election, how can he win it (despite what the polls are showing), and just see what freedom of thought and speech can build. Thank you for your precious time to read my first non-fiction book, Trump: Trust the Plan.

Table of Content

CHAPTER 1
Why (am I) Here

True or False. Can election prediction be as easy as saying true or false? Well, according to Professor Allan Lichtman 13 Keys Presidential Predictor, yes, we can. He has been right since 1984 and has tested his model or 13 questions for the last 120 years. He has been right every time. Even in 2016, he was right. Yes, one of the rare forecasts which actually called out Donald Trump winning the 2016 election. He is a lifetime, Democrat. In one of his interviews, he spoke about the question works if personal bias is kept out. Well, keeping his personal bias (???) out, he has announced to the world that President Donald Trump will lose 2020. He will lose this election to Democratic presidential nominee Joe Biden. Will even if Joe steps down now, Trump will still loose. This made me think. Can he be right? I am following Donald Trump for over two decades now and a watcher of US politics. But if an American citizen, I would have identified myself as a Democrat.

Yes, I am not an American citizen. But have spoken when needed and shared my opinion on America at different times. A decade ago, I wanted Barrack Obama to win. I wanted Al Gore to win. I never liked George Bush (Senior or Junior). And Bill Clinton was a charmer. Democrat, I was by the heart. And I fit the bill if I was in the United States (as a citizen). An immigrant Asian from India. Dark brown skin. Postgraduate in Science / Management and potentially earning in a six-figure number. I would be for globalization and have a soft corner for socialism and understand leftist policies as time went on. I would live the American Dream with a flair of leftist ideas. But this did not happen.

As time went on, I started reading, hearing voices from all three sides: the liberal sides, the conservative side, and the central side. There were things l like for all sides. But the most important attributes for me were less government intervention, social equity, freedom of speech, and, more important, freedom to think. The media also changed. Slowly there were less centralist channels. Most channels moved towards the bipolar opposite of each other. Discourse should be cherished. Because if we cannot come together to have a discussion, we cannot ensure that freedom and growth are protected. As I read more, I heard voices from

Conservatives, Libertarians, Centralists, and other moderates, my views began to evolve. The discussion with different minds was allowed a balanced perspective to be seen. Not everyone is right.

Similarly, not everyone is wrong. I do not share that guns should be held by an individual or communities on a broad scale. Still, I am ready to understand that it is part of the United States Constitution and linked to the ethos*. A difference in opinion should not mean that one cannot work with another. The mainstream did not help further. They had their narratives, and I began to switch off from them. But the quest continued.

And in this quest for understanding, views led to scrutinizing things more. President Obama got the Nobel Peace Prize. There should be an end to the endless wars. But Libya (especially Benghazi) showed to be something is definitely not right. Then the rise of ISIS. How in this age of Satellite, live feeds, and superior weapons a terrorist organization can be born, get weapons, get funding (and sell oil) and do such dastardly deals. There was supposed to peace, and yet it was more of the same. I saw certain Democrats calling out for socialism. To be honest, Bernie's views charmed me for a while. But the question then kept coming back to me. What if the United States changes, and instead of saving it falls? As a history enthusiast, I have read civilization rise, reach their zenith and fall. Is the United States on it fall naturally or been forced by certain internal fifth column elements? The rabbit hole for such discussion will go on. But in the crux, I saw freedom and liberty going away. I saw considerable government control and surveillance rising. Who will police the police?

This is the time Candidate Trump spoke about the slogan "Make America Great Again." He was the ultimate outsider. Can he create an impact like Ross Perot to give a different view, or will he be more of the same? I read his books in college in the 90s. Followed him a bit but did not watch his reality show. I knew he was a man who loved America. His plan was one, the United STATES of AMERICA. This was about the future of the nation. It is about restoring faith in the country. And if the USA falls, then there is a strong probability Democracy and liberty will fall across the planet. That is why I felt his point of Making (and now Keeping) America Great was important.

---

*The Second Amendment was around not letting a tyrannical government take control, and for safekeeping, defense, and protection of the individual and family. As a reader of history, I do remember gun confiscation by the Nazis as part of their plan to gain a stranglehold on the country, among other ways, liberty was taken away.

Why does the United States need to be Kept Great?

Two books that I had read more than three decades ago as a young boy were George Orwell's 1984 and Animal Farm. And later read Huxley's A Brave New World. All three have a common connection. The connection of control. Control to keep the common citizenry under control (through different means). In short, it was about more Government, till it moves to total government. History has shown us that when a great power falls, another is waiting for the wing, which rises to take its place. Even the United States gained prominence once the British Empire declined. Britain rose after France fell. France rose after the Spanish empire's fall, and before it was (Oranges) Netherland Royalty. These are the trends of the past. So, if the United States falls, who will take its place? Yes, you guessed it right, China.

Now let's think if it is China, so what? Now would you want to move to a communist-run country where individual liberty and human rights are limited? Where freedom of thought is not allowed, and social scoring determines the life ones live. This is a danger which is clear and present. This is one strong reason for me to say this "For democracy and liberty to survive, the United States needs to be great and strong." And only Donald Trump as President Trump can counter this. So, from MAGA, it must be Keep America Great in 2020. If China wins, then where will be liberty, freedom of speech, and human rights go?

This is a war of ideas for the future of the planet. This war is carried by narratives. And the only way to fight these narratives is to share counter-narratives. This is why I am writing. As the narrative has been built is for President Trump to lose and if he wins, then cast doubt on the victory. Then the opponents of President Trump (and Liberty) will carry out a Color Revolution (more in Chapter 12).

Coming back to Professor Allan Lichtman. We will see the details of each of his keys (Chapter 4&5). The keys are:

Party Mandate | Contest | Incumbency |Third party | Short-term economy | Long-term economy |Policy change | Social unrest | Scandal | Foreign/military failure | Foreign/military success | Incumbent (party) charisma | Challenger (party) charisma

Before going details into the keys, let us first delve a bit into Prediction and Predication science.

CHAPTER 2
Prediction Science

Who can see the future? Is there a crystal-ball where we can know what is happening? Nostradamus, Baba Vanga, or other soothsayers across history spoke of the future. They spoke, and we interpreted. Our interpretation of their words had various stories. And most of it was clear after an event happened. We joined the dots. That is what the human brain is good at, connecting dots. What we see is human intuition and pattern recognition in play here. We now have the science and technology power to find and study patterns in large numbers. There is a saying which I heard before that "history does not repeat but often rhymes." Once we understand the rhymes of the past, we can take a look into the future. A glimpse can be seen, which can help us better prepare and plan. This is another way to see behavior science in action. When I think of prediction as a science, a lot comes to mind. But to focus here in this book, let me look into political prediction.

When I think of political prediction, the first thing which comes to my mind is the consulting Simulmatics Corporation. It was started its operation in 1959, and its first significant project was the Presidential elections in 1960, which JFK won. It was hired by the Democratic Party in 1959 (now thing about Cambridge Analytica news now). What Simulmatics did was find out what is going in voters' minds using pattern recognition techniques via computer simulation and building on previous data. So, sort of big data was used. They created a model for the US electorate, dividing them into around 480 district types of voters. And these messaging techniques may play a role for JFK to win by one of the slimmest margins in terms of the popular vote. A difference of 0.2%. Needless to say, a controversy was created as sections of the media were calling the dangers of how voters were hacked using "What-If Men." This term What-If Men came about as the scientist of this corporation (Simulmatics) worked on endless simulation creating "What-If" scenarios. Scenarios could predict how would a human (voter) behave to which message and situation. JFK was trailing Nixon in the summer. And as the history books have sown, Simulmatics suggested ideas on how to change the narrative – Championing the Civil Rights (African

American voters), Freedom of Religion (Conservative), and do Televised Debates (new-age audience). 0.2% was the difference. And victory using such techniques led to more questions than answers. Yet this science was expanded with companies, specialists, and unique propriety tools and techniques been developed. To forecast any election result, some of the commonly used methods are

- Polling questions carried out to potential voters using market research techniques (which means correct sampling)
- Average of various research polls carried out

But they are ways where pollsters have developed different techniques. One such approach is Professor Allan Lichtman's 13 Questions. Before going there, let us see other techniques or practices to determine who will win the election.

When I started looking for different examples, a wide range of logical and interpretational models came. Some made sense, and some did not make sense. Well, those who did not make sense, like an Octopus picking up the winner, I will not discuss but will list in the section of the book called – "Just for Fun." Do check it towards the end of the book. Now for the examples which stood out (not necessary used in every election) are the following:

- **Primary Elections**: These are elections in which voters (affiliated/ registered to a party) select one candidate to represent them at an election. Using this as a metric, there is a model developed called The Primary Model. This statistical model correctly predicted the results of the Presidential election in 2016. The call was made in early 2016 that Donald Trump has an 87% certainty of defeating Hillary Clinton and 99% certainty to defeat Bernie Sanders. We know what happened. This model was introduced in 1996. With slight modification, it has correctly predicted the winner of the popular vote in five Presidential elections. When back-tested till 1912 (the year Primaries were introduced), it failed only once in 1960. What struck me is that the model predicted that if Donald Trump was not nominated, the Republicans would lose, and Hillary Clinton would win. And if Bernie Sanders would have been the candidate for the Democrats, then even Marco Rubio would have won the election. Now that did not happen. It was Trump vs. Clinton. History was made.

- **Face of Candidate**: This study looked if there was something like a facial competence. The objective was to understand if there were snap judgments carried out based on the candidate's face. This was carried out on the Primaries elections in 2008 for the Democrats and Republicans. When we look into the prediction for Democrats, Obama and Hillary Clinton came on the top. And Hillary scored above. In fact, Hillary was ahead in Popular vote when Obama clinched the nomination. Yup, she was ahead (though in final Primary count, she was 41,622 behind). Now, if we do a facial competence rating between Trump and Biden, what will come up. I leave that thought to you.

- **Candidates Biographical Information**: This model's developer took 59 (or 58) biographical variables to create a "bio-index." The candidate who is rated highest in these variables will win the popular vote. This model was tested for 29 US Presidential elections (1896-2009). When validated with results, 27 out of 29 times, the model picked the popular vote winner. The model failed to determine the popular vote winner in 1976 (Gerald Ford lost to Jimmy Carter) and 1992 (George Bush lost to Bill Clinton). So close to 93% hit rate. The primary use of this model, according to the developer, is to help parties shortlist and select the right candidate. The model used the Republican candidates in the Primaries to see who can win against Obama. It picked Rick Perry. Yup, the governor of Texas and United States Secretary of Energy. We know what happened. He could not win the Primaries. When I further checked how this model worked for 2016, this is what I found. Their model picked Hillary Clinton to win a landslide against Donald Trump (accurate as it is a Popular vote model). Still, she would be tied with Ted Cruz. But as there is a saying, the devil is in the details – the matchup between Trump and Hillary showed that Hillary would win 58.3% of the popular vote. They were off by over 10 points.

Over the year's prediction science has evolved. But its soul depends on understanding human behavior. These models work on the past data, candidates' metrics, and questions asked to potential voters (and non-citizens in some cases). One came type in all the data into the computer, but understanding human behavior needs more than technology and methodology. These people who make the predictions, which I like to call Statidatastics Priests, have their rules set. These soothsayers or Statidatastics Priests place science, math, and technology behind the results they call out. They use a set of rules they understand and develop it further towards a conclusion. All these conclusions are in black and white with a hint of probability. But such results can be used as a narrative controller. In a world of psyops, data can be used for social engineering. These Statidatastics Priests are messengers. They believe in themselves and talk about their results. The model they build works based on the data they get. But what happens when it does not get the data it needs and data changes. The voice of people is heard. What we have seen from JFK's times to now, the questions of the past remain today. Can big data and computation power be used to rig elections? These are tools. Tools of influence and mind hacking. Anything too much can be again wrong. And we have seen some examples of how predictions have gone wrong. In the next chapter, I look into more about this.

CHAPTER 3
Predictions Gone Crazy

Who can see the future? So when does election prediction go wrong? Traditional polling always works during the elections of the state. Many organizations, survey groups, political experts predict the result of the polls. These predictions are based on the ground realities, turn over rate, people's thinking during the election, their previous track record, etc. Many famous polling companies go on the ground level and do the surveys by asking them which candidate you will vote for? For example, Gallup, CBS News, Harris, etc. Most times, these predictions are almost accurate, but sometimes it is different. Here the most recent example is the 2016 election of the USA. Conclusion This was the election where many political experts, pundits, polling companies, and survey groups failed. The results were totally different in the opposite direction. Even the Gallup, with 80 years of polling experience, failed in their prediction. Similarly, the New York Times, Princeton election consortium, and Pew research center was unable to predict the 2016 results.

History of Election Prediction in the United States

Political experts, polling companies, and survey groups always consider the previous elections. When we check the record of 20 years, we can only analyze the five presidential elections. The most important thing is changing facts, technologies, ground realities, the mentality of people. If we go back to 1990-2000, then the ground facts, technologies were totally different. Social media was not that prevalent in the past. So we cannot depend on the previous record. I think this was the mistake that everyone made in the 2016 election. For example, Nate Silver (From New York Times, FiveThirtyEight), who accurately predicted the 2012 elections, got it wrong in 2016. In the 2016 election, they claimed that Clinton has 71.4% chances to win the election. Other experts also got it wrong. These experts go wrong in the 2016 election, and the person who does not have any record of public service won the election. The 2016 election will be seen in history as the most significant error in election predictions.

Everyone thinks about how these competent institutions and professional political analysts and experts failed in their predictions. All these institutions and experts have an impressive track record regarding their election predictions. So what happened in the 2016 election that they all failed in their forecast? The reason is that they all analyzed the previous polls, voting rate, psychology of voters, etc.. Still, they ignored the critical factor of amplifying reach via technologies and social media. Trump and his team were very professional and active in social media; they approached every voter in a modern way and conveyed their slogans. This election set history in the USA and told everyone that this can also happen in the polls. Some examples of wrong predictions:

- 1936: US: Roosevelt Wins Again
- 1945: UK: Churchill Wins War, loses election against Labour
- 1948: US: Dewey defeats Truman
- 1960: US: JFK defeats Nixon
- 2016: US: We know what happened

Why were so many of experts, Polling companies went wrong in the 2016 US election:

Many experts give different reasons, e.g., low turnover, people did not cast a vote, tempering, etc., but the ground reality is different from it. The most important thing that Donald Trump adopted was "digital-first" his team used social media apps for their campaigning. Hillary spent more than $200 million on TV ads, Commercials, advertisements, etc. Trump spent half on it and spent $275 million on Facebook and Instagram.

The other thing was the overconfidence by Hillary. This was the reason that, according to PolitiFact, Clinton spent less time in the campaign, and Trump spent 70% of the time. And for the voters, Hillary was a less popular candidate. They were close elections in certain states. And Hillary had not visited such states, like Pennsylvania, thinking the blue wall would hold. It did not. Candidate Trump pushed the messages – JOBS! MAGA!

CHAPTER 4
Allan Lichtman's Thirteen Keys

True or False. Can election prediction be as easy as saying true or false? Well, "it depends." According to a historian at American University in Washington, D.C, the answers seem to be yes. His name is Dr. Allan Lichtman. In 1981, he and a Russian (yes, you read it right RUSSIAN!) seismologist and mathematical geophysicist Vladimir Keilis-Borok developed a model to predict Presidential Elections. The name of the model – The Keys to the White House. Vladimir Keilis-Borok was the founder of the International Institute of Earthquake Prediction Theory and Mathematical Geophysics in Moscow. This prediction system has certain inspiration from earthquake research. The thinking is around the understanding that structural factors beneath the surface are more critical in earthquake prediction than the factors the surface. When we think of these structural factors as events that the electorate feels for, there can be seismic change resulting in volcanic activity (explosion) of voting out the incumbent or Party in power. To cover these events, thirteen questions where framed. These questions were varied and coved the following topics.

Party Mandate | Contest | Incumbency | Third-party | Short-term economy | Long-term economy |Policy change | Social unrest | Scandal | Foreign/military failure | Foreign/military success | Incumbent (party) charisma | Challenger (party) charisma

I will come to the details of the questions within these topics soon. When this model was tested by Lichtman between 1860 to 1980, and six or more questions go against the Party in power or incumbent, their challenger wins. Seeing this, Lichtman started applying it to elections from that period. Sometimes he announced his results months before the main Presidential election. And few times years. In both cases, what was seen, his prediction has been called right. The "Right" here was based on the objective – a popular vote, which later changed to the electoral college vote. More on this later in the chapter.

When I look at the questions, these questions are excellent and balanced. It speaks around governance. If the governance is good, then the challenger loses. Isn't this what citizens need? Well, true, but with changing dynamics, what I one group of voters may feel a strong True, the other voters may feel a neutral or weak true to the factors. This may be due to a personal perspective or bias or point of view. If these voters of particular attributes are in substantial numbers, then it can swing a state. And this is impacting the electoral college votes. For 2020 Allan Lichtman has called the election for Biden or the challenger (in case Biden steps down). Yes, President Trump is going to lose. Or is he? Let us see the questions and Professor Allan Lichtman's interpretation of the voter's structural elements, aka factors. The following is a list of true-false statements used to determine who will win the 2020 presidential election:

Q	Factor	Question	Lichtman's Rating
1	Party Mandate	The incumbent's Party gained House seats between midterm elections	FALSE
2	Contest	There is no primary contest for the incumbent's Party	TRUE
3	Incumbency	The incumbent is running for reelection	TRUE
4	Third-party	There is no third-party challenger	TRUE
5	Short-term economy	The short-term economy is strong	FALSE
6	Long-term economy	The long-term economic growth during the incumbent's term has been as good as the past two terms	FALSE
7	Policy change	The incumbent has made major changes to national policy	TRUE
8	Social unrest	There is no social unrest during the incumbent's term	FALSE
9	Scandal	The incumbent is untainted by scandal	FALSE
10	Foreign/military failure	The incumbent has no major foreign or military failures abroad	TRUE
11	Foreign/military success	The incumbent has a major foreign or military success abroad	FALSE
12	Incumbent (Party) charisma	The incumbent is charismatic –	FALSE
13	Challenger (Party) charisma	The challenger is uncharismatic –	TRUE

You saw six active keys for the incumbent (President Trump), which means he loses the election.

Let us read now what Lichtman said about the keys:

- "The Keys show that elections are not horse races in which candidates surge ahead or fall behind on the campaign trail, with pollsters keeping score."
- "Rather, a pragmatic American electorate chooses a President according to the performance of the Party holding the White House as measured by the consequential events and episodes of a term — economic boom and bust, foreign policy successes and failures, social unrest, scandal, and policy innovation.

Fair enough. So now let us go back a few years. A little over a decade. The year around the 2008 period. I wanted to check what Allan Lichtman called out for President Barrack Obama during his first run and his rerun in 2012. The details are there in the below table and compared with Trump's first run in 2016 and the latest 2020 call.

Keys	1	2	3	4	5	6	7	8	9	10	11	12	13	Outcome
2008	T	F	T	F	T	F	T	F	T	T	T	T	T	9 (T) Obama
2012	T	T	T	T	T	F	T	T	T	T	T	T	T	10 (T) Obama
2016	F	T	F	F	T	T	F	T	T	T	F	F	F	7 (F) Trump
2020	F	T	T	T	F	F	T	F	F	T	F	F	T	6 (T) Challenger

It was 9 keys for Obama in the first run and 10 keys during his rerun. This was not surprising for me, and I would have believed it if I would have seen it during that period. Why? Because I felt Obama was a coming of peace and savior of Humanity after war-mongering President George Walker Bush. And I believe what the media said. As I read more and understood different views, my thinking expanded. When I researched the US's political issues during the Obama period, there were so many topics I was not aware of. The media did a good job not sharing with the world. And if something was told, it was never amplified. And now, President Trump gets up to 95% negative coverage. This is not balanced. Something is wrong.

So, does it mean Allan Lichtman is right, and President Trump will be voted out? For that lets us see now if Allan Lichtman was ever wrong. Into the fine print now.

Has Allan Lichtman been Wrong Earlier?

Yin and Yang. Right and Wrong. True or False. When we see the universe's laws, one thing that happens with a hundred percent probability is that something will go wrong. For Allan Lichtman to say that all will go according to plan and he is right, I cannot digest it. Not because I am a fan of President Trump, but I think one should look at the broader picture to see the citizens' views and how the polls are skewed along with the claustrophobic narrative of the mainstream media against the President. More on this later, but in this chapter, I wanted to check the history of his prediction and check the fine print.

It is true that according to him and the results he has called since the 1984 elections, Professor Allan Lichtman is right. But there is fine print to it. The model has changed over the years. It has been tweaked. Plus, I am not sure if the results on the 120 years of back-testing he carried out have been challenged on each key level. The challenge of qualitative analysis can be calls taken based on the data placed without opposing data been presented. (Maybe he has done, but I am happy to talk with him on this and hear him out). For now, I will see the election results since 1984.

The Presidents who have won the elections during the active period of the model have been six. They are – Regan, Bush (Sr), Clinton, Bush, Obama, and Trump. So, nine elections, he has been right. Or is it so. In the 2000 election, he called 'Al Gore' as the winner. Now how is this possible. The model till that period was only for the popular vote. And according to the popular vote, George Bush had lost to Al Gore and won the Electoral College. Same case in Donald Trump vs. Hillary Clinton case. If that is the case, why is the media always shouting the headline that the Professor never got it wrong? See a sample below:

- Professor with perfect prediction record forecasts Donald Trump loss to Joe Biden
- 13 keys spell doom for Trump: Allan Lichtman
- Professor Predicts that Biden Will Beat Trump in Election

These and others called had the same tone and narrative - Presidential forecaster who got every election result right, has predicted Trump's loss. So, is it right without going into the fine print?

The media is also right in a way, as the model till then was calling out for the popular vote. So, Professor Allan Lichtman is right and wrong at the same time. This is like the Schrodinger Cat thought experiment. In this thought experiment, a paradox is discussed. The experiment states that if one places a cat within a box with something that can kill the cat, and after we seal it, one would not know if the cat is dead or alive until we open the box. So, you see something is wrong. The 120 back-tested elections can be fixed, and the model can be tweaked. I read an article that said the Lichtman model predicted Trump winning the popular vote in 2016. According to this article, when challenged, Lichtman changed his model interpretation. The article rightly said that any interpretation and elements must be established before the election and not after. We have seen that in earlier elections, there was a change in the model. So, my case is that this is not bullet-proof.

The article questioned the validity of the results based on the book's details, which Alan Lichtman wrote. The 2008 book, The Keys to the White House: A Surefire Guide to Predicting the Next President (Rowman & Littlefield Publishers, 2008), spoke that his model predicts the popular vote winner. The book mentions that only the national votes are taken and not votes in each individual state. There were examples given in the book wherein three elections since 1860. His model predicted the popular vote winner, but they did not get the electoral college victory. These elections were –

- 1876: Democrat Samuel J. Tilden won the popular vote, lost to Republican Rutherford B. Hayes

- 1888: Democrat Grover Cleveland won the popular vote lost to Republican Benjamin Harrison

- 2000 Democrat Al Gore won the popular vote but lost to Republican George W. Bush

In these three elections, the book had the points the Keys accurately predicted the popular vote winner. Thus, his model works. But popular vote and not Presidential elections. In such a case, this model should be labeled a popular vote winner and not Presidential forecaster as the media calls it to be. The author wrote to Lichtman about this and did get a reply from him. Lichtman said he never said anything about the electoral college or popular vote. Still, only Donald Trump would win the presidency. In the public domain, Lichtman's statement after the Al Gore election in 2000 is that the "Keys" predict only the national popular vote and not the states. If this is the case, then his model and what the media is saying is wrong. So, his model is fallible. I have summarized this discussion in the following table.

	2000	**2016**
Popular Vote Winner	Al Gore	Hillary Clinton
Model Allan Lichtman's Model Pick	Al Gore	Donald Trump
2008 edition Book The Keys to the White House: A Surefire Guide to Predicting the Next President		"The Keys to the White House focus on national concerns such as economic performance, policy initiatives, social unrest, presidential scandal, and successes and failures in foreign affairs. Thus, **they predict only the national popular vote** and **not the vote within individual states**."

Thus, the model was wrong in 2000 or in 2016. It cannot be right in both cases. When the media claim saying the Professor always gets it right in Predicting Presidential candidates is wrong. When we look at this model, I see it more like a heuristic model. What does heuristic mean? It is a technique where one approaches problem-solving using a methodology, which is more around approximation to reach an answer when timelines are less. These are flexible techniques that are intuitive and give us quick decisions using mental shortcuts. The questions are true and false questions, which are based on available information. But with the change of mediums of communication – and so many filters around; what is the interpretation of this information. One may see data of economy and the stock market down, but if the employment rate is high and there is a positive outlook among different voters, will they not vote for the incumbent Party or President. This is where I feel the need to study how the KEYS will work in the battleground state. Based on whatever I have followed and read, there are 12 states which will decide the future. These states are Florida, Pennsylvania, Michigan, Minnesota, Ohio, Wisconsin, New Hampshire, Nevada, Maine, North Carolina, Arizona, and Texas. And a 13th state (California) will be necessary for gaining in the popular vote. Suppose we take the total popular vote across the United States. In that case, two places are skewed heavily towards Democrats – California and New York. When I see the last four Presidential elections, this is how the vote breaks down looked.

States	Democrat Votes	Republican Votes	Vote Difference The gap for Trump and Republicans	Democrats Votes to Total National Democrats Votes %
California 2012	7,854,285	4,839,958	- 30,14,327	**11.9%**
California 2016	8,753,788	4,483,810	- 42,69,978	**13.3%**
New York 2012	4,485,877	2,490,496	- 19,95,381	**6.8%**
New York 2016	4,556,124	2,819,534	- 17,36,590	**6.9%**
New York + California 2012	1,23,40,162	73,30,454	- 50,09,708	**18.7%**
New York + California 2016	1,33,09,912	73,03,344	- 60,06,568	**20.2%**

What you read in the table above shows how much is the dependency of Democrats on two states. In the 2016 election, 20.2% of Democratic votes came from these two states. This point has been highlighted by Allan Lichtman has mentioned. In an interview, I saw he elaborated on it. He said that there will be 5-6 million votes for Democrats always. This is due to two states California and New York. When we consider certain cities in these two states, most of the contributions come from these locations. How these five to six million voters react to the key will also be critical. A shift in these votes will make a change in the populate vote total. These 5-6 million voters are almost 5% of the total ballots taking an average of the last two Presidential elections. But there is always a narrative push by mainstream media.

Saying this, I still wanted to see how the keys would work when I go into the fine print and take each key separately and compare it with what Professor Lichtman says as his reason. Let's now see the individual keys.

CHAPTER 5
The Keys

Our brain is trained to think linearly. We are comfortable to think about addition and subtraction. Given a choice, it is yes, and no answer would be better. But as we have progressed, complexity has increased. There are more choices, and it is not a binary option anymore. What human minds need to see is exponential. Allan Lichtman has been called the man who could see Trump winning in 2016 (and the President sent him a congratulatory note later). Another man was called early. It was from Michael Moore. He said to quote him, "Trump's election is going to be the biggest f#$@ you ever recorded in human history." Now 2020, be part 2. According to Professor Lichtman, the answer is 'No. President Trump will not win.'

Based on his Keys framework. The following will be the rating: **Incumbent**: 6 keys, and **Challenger**: 7 keys. Trump loses.

Key	Key Category	Call
1	Party Mandate	False
2	Contest	True
3	Incumbency	True
4	Third-Party	True
5	Short Term Economy	False
6	Long Term Economy	False
7	Policy Change	True
8	Social Unrest	False
9	Scandal	False
10	Foreign or Military Failure	True
11	Foreign or Military Success	False
12	Incumbent Charisma	False
13	Challenger Charisma	True

This rating is something I disagree with. So, in this chapter, we will look into the 13 keys independently. But what I would like to share with my readers is how I see the 13 keys. I do not see them as always independent. There is a connection between the keys, and the affirmation strength of one key can be higher than the others. By affirmation strength, I mean the importance of the key to the individual. As I said below, the keys are like the national mandate. But the battle is in thirteen states, and the citizens in those states will determine the national outcome. This does not mean the other states are not as important as this election; winning the popular vote with a higher mandate becomes especially important. Now let me show how I see the framework linked together.

Key Canvas:

Our voting decision depends on multiple attributes. Some of us can vote based on one issue and some on numerous topics. These attributes' strength will depend on how it impacts me and what inference I can draw from what I see and hear. Based on this, I will be motivated to vote for, against, or do not vote at all. Before we go into the keys' details, I will place a few notes on the connect and linkages I see. To understand how the 13 Keys impacts, I made a canvas of what I see:

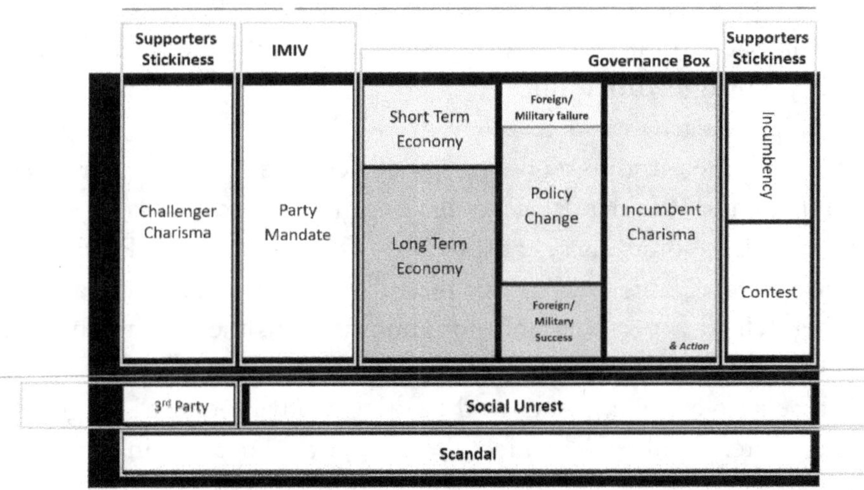

There are two zones — the top zone is about individual, administration, and action. The bottom zone is about events which either external or out-of-control. So let's see the top zone first. In this zone, there are ten keys in play here under four categories of decision impactors.

- **Supporter Stickiness** (Incumbent)
  Keys Active: Incumbency | Contest | Incumbent Charisma
  The keys in this category show how united the incumbent party core voters are. If there is aggressive primary competition, then there can be a loss of certain voters. This we saw in 2016, where a certain number of Bernie voters did not turn up or voted for Trump or the third Party. In a close election, this can make an impact. If the Charisma is strong, it will create a broader base ground worker who will canvas across the constituency and amplify their candidate message. This will bring independents and other party voters Example - #WalkAwayMovement (Brandon Straka)
- **Governance Box**:
  Keys Active: Policy Change | Long Term Economy | Short Term Economy | Foreign Military Success | Foreign Military Failure |Incumbent Charisma (& Action)
  Various keys here impact the governance quality of the administration. It is intertwined and connected. Policies bring out the impact on the economy, foreign affairs, and military matters.
- **Party Voting Motivation**:
  Keys Active: Party Mandate
  It is seen the turnout in congressional elections is often lesser when compared to Presidential elections. But there is also a linkage of how much the voters are satisfied by the incumbent President's performance. This can be seen the following way — The impact the voter felt at a personal and community level, the incumbent and challenger Party's message stimulus. Based on this, what inference can he derive? All this leads to the voting motivation level. To go out and vote. Vote for which Party. Vote keeping in mind a Congressional candidate or the President in mind.

- **Supporter Stickiness** (Challenger):
  Suppose the incumbent is a great communicator pushing the right buttons in the voter's mind. In that case, this creates a problem for the incumbent. This then becomes a clash between not only ideas but also of personalities.

The bottom zone is impacted by events that unfold over time. Once activated, these events can lead to a change of public opinion perception, often leading to a change in how a person is voting. The three Key in play here are:

- 3rd Party Vote
- Social Unrest
- Scandal

To make an objective view, we need to connect the various attributes impacting the Keys and make a decision for the future. This is the important word - The future. For the future and not the past. The past is a road we have walked, and the future is where we want to go as a nation. If our ability to reason or see things objectively is destroyed, dimmed down, or silenced, many make emotional decisions. These decisions are often is done without taking logic into consideration. For me, this is the real election interference. Mind Hacking to create a socially engineered result. This is a topic for another day. For now, we will focus on how to look at the keys. What you will see ahead is a set of 13 sub-chapters. Each chapter deals with an individual key. We start with the definition of the key, the rating that Allan Lichtman gave, his interpretation of why the key is the score that way, and my interpretation and scoring. At the end of the chapter, there will be continuous tracking of the keys scores. The following structure you will see towards the end of the page of the sub-chapter

Allan Lichtman Rating: True/ False | **Clark Rating**: True/ False or ?

President Trump *Active Keys*: L# vs. C# (#S1 + #S2 + #S3)

The first line is around the rating which Allan Lichtman and which I provide. A True call will get a "1" score, and a False call will get a "0" score. I am also providing a 0.5 score for some keys, which I see as a mixed impact Key. This will be written as "?" in that part. The "0.5" rating is vital as such keys can resonate in the swing states more. This election is about the electoral college votes and WINNING the popular vote in a large number. So, the "0.5" rating be useful for guiding and tacking such keys.

The second line calls out the count of President Trump Active Keys. The number of total active keys is updated as we move ahead from Key 1 to Key 13. The acronyms and definition for this second line are the following:

- L#: Count of TRUE which Allan Lichtman made (Will be 1)
- C#: Count of TRUE which I have taken (Can be 1 or 0.5)
- Within the brackets, three kinds of total values will be shown:
    - S1: My TRUE rating, which resonates with Lichtman
    - S2: My TRUE rating, which does not resonate with Lichtman
    - S3: My TRUE rating, which can impact popular vote and, in some cases, the swing states

This is again a point of view, which can be discussed and challenged. For now, let's see the 2020 Keys in detail.

Key #1
Party Mandate

After the midterm elections, the incumbent Party holds more seats in the U.S. House of Representatives than after the previous midterm elections.

Allan Lichtman Rating: False
"Republicans lost the U.S. House midterms in 2018."

It is clear that the Democrats have done well during the 2018 midterm and taken back the house. The final count was 235 for Republicans, and 199 for Democrats. This was a momentum shift from the 2016 elections. As per data shown, there was X number of counties that had voted for Trump but now had a Democratic win. On the other side, X counties that voted for Clinton were won by Republicans. But I wanted to look this at the historical context. What has been seen is the incumbent President loses the house. This has happened 9 out of 11 times in the last 42 years. Details in the table below.

House Election Year	Party Holding Presidency	Incumbent Gain/Loss Of Seats	Next Presidency	Key Result Relationship
1978	Democrat	-15	Republican	Correlated
1982	Republican	-26	Republican	Not Correlated
1986	Republican	-5	Republican	Not Correlated
1990	Republican	-8	Democrat	Correlated
1994	Democrat	-54	Democrat	Not Correlated
1998	Democrat	5	Republican	Not Correlated
2002	Republican	8	Republican	Correlated
2006	Republican	-30	Democrat	Correlated
2010	Democrat	-63	Democrat	Not Correlated
2014	Democrat	-13	Republican	Correlated
2018	Republican	-42	??	??

So, what we can see here is that there is not always a correlation. Five times out of the last ten scenario (1978 to 2014), it has failed. This means five times either the incumbent held or a new President took over during ten presidential elections (1980 to 2016). That is a fifty percent failure rate. The number of Presidential Elections where the congress's loss led to the Party's change was 5 times the last 9 elections. The Key is not a perfect marker. Now I need to dig more into the data. The objective was to understand the motivation of the base and voters. Now at the 2018 election, there was a loss of 42 seats for Republicans

- 30: Republicans lost re-election to Democrats
- 13: Republican seats won by Democrats
- 3: Democratic seats won by Republicans
- 29 seat loss in 11 Democratic-run states

One strong reason is turnout. The turnout of 50.3% is the highest in a US Mid-Term election since 1914. This is voter motivation to come out and vote. But there were close races. Out of 89 races where the margin of victory was under 10%, 19 Republican seats, which flipped to Democrats, had less than 5%. Yes, 19 seats could have gone the other way. The voter's motivation in Republican was less in these seats. There can be local factors involved. Now to see if this can impact the Presidential election, lets us visit the 12 states:

Republic Loss	No Change	Loss
Florida (2) |Pennsylvania (4) Michigan (2) |North Carolina (1) | Maine (1) |Texas (2)	Ohio |Minnesota | Wisconsin | Nevada |New Hampshire	12 Seats in 5 core states

12 States for Nation to Decide and History to be impacted:
Florida, Pennsylvania, Ohio, Michigan, North Carolina, Arizona, Minnesota, Wisconsin, Nevada, New Hampshire, Maine & Texas

Going through these details – not a strong correlation (5/9) and less loss of seats in the 12 states, the Key for me is a weak False. Or a 0.5.

Allan Lichtman Rating: False | **Clark Rating:** (?)

President Trump *Active Keys*: 0 vs. 0.5 (0 + 0 + 0.5)

Key #2
Contest

Contest: There is no serious contest for the incumbent party nomination.

Allan Lichtman Rating: True
"No Republicans challenged Trump."

As an incumbent, President Trump did not have a Primary challenger. Though they were other candidates who challenged him (do not remember their names). The votes which Donald Trump won were over eighteen million votes (18,159,752). When we compare this number of votes with his 2016 Republican Presidential Primary votes, it is thirty % higher. Wow. Really. I had to check up the numbers again and again. Candidate Trump's number in 2016 was 14,015,993 votes in a completed Primary process. If the Republican 2020 primary had concluded, the number of votes would have crossed over twenty million. Why is this important? See below the table below

Candidates	Votes 2016 Primaries	Candidates	Votes 2020 Primaries
Trump	1,40,15,993	Trump	1,81,59,752
Hillary	1,69,17,853	Biden	1,84,48,092
2016 Primary Republican Votes	~ 30631637	2016 Primary Democratic Votes	~35828495
2020 Primary Republican Votes	~31216021	2020 Primary Democratic Votes	~ 19320941

What you can see here is the Republican bases are more engaged in 2016. And in the non-active Primaries election cycle for Republicans, turning out in large numbers shows the motivation. This Key in my conclusion this is a True

Allan Lichtman Rating: True | **Clark Rating:** True

President Trump *Active Keys*: 1 vs. 1.5 (1 + 0 + 0.5)

Key #3
Incumbency

The incumbent is running for reelection. The incumbent party candidate is the sitting President.

Allan Lichtman Rating: True
"Doesn't look like he's stepping down."

As an incumbent, President Trump did not have a Primary challenger. Though they were other candidates who challenged him (do not remember their names). The votes which Donald Trump won were over 18 million votes (18,159,752). The total vote cast was close to 30 million. When we compare this number of votes with his 2016 Republican Presidential Primary votes, it is 30 % higher. Wow. Really. I had to check up the numbers again and again. Candidate Trump's number in 2016 had 14,015,993 votes in a completed Primary process. In 2020 votes was 18,159,752. It could have been higher, maybe close to 20 million, if the Pandemic did not hit. Numbers make a difference.

Why is this important? When I checked primary votes for incumbent Presidents, this is what I found:

- Obama (2012): 6.1 million
- George Bush (2004): 7.8 million
- Bill Clinton (1996): 9.7 million
- Ronald Regan (1984): 6.4 million

Do you see these numbers? This shows strong base support for the feet on the ground movement for Trump. This means amplification of positive noise for Trump and how motivated the base is.
Keep these factors, the rating is a "Strong True."

Allan Lichtman Rating: True | **Clark Rating:** True

President Trump *Active Keys*: 2 vs. 2.5 (2 + 0 + 0.5)

Key #4
Third-Party

There is no major third-party challenge.

Allan Lichtman Rating: True
"Despite claims by Kanye West to be running, this is a two-party race."

Something is not apparent here. If there is a third-party candidate or a group of third, fourth, or fifth candidates clumped together taking votes away, who is impacted. Is it the incumbent or the challenger? Are Republicans going to be hit like Ross Perot in 1992? Or is it the Democrat going to hit like the Green party in 2000? Alternatively, going back in time, Nixon won the Presidency with 56 % electoral votes and 43.4% popular vote (his Dem opponent had 42.7% popular vote). There was a strong 3rd party candidate in George Wallace in that race who won 46 electoral votes and 13.5 % of popular votes.

I started looking at the election results from 2016. Overall, Libertarian Party candidate Johnson and Green Party candidate Stein won 4.4% of the populate vote together in terms of votes. This is significant as Trump did not win the popular vote. So, a weaker third parties challenge could have swung a few states towards Hillary. Was this the case?

I started looking at the swing states then. The focus was to see where the margin of victory is smaller than the third party vote share. I just looked at those states Trump won.

State (electoral college votes)	Trump Vote %	Hillary Vote %	Vote Share % Difference (Votes)	3rd Party Vote %	Total Others %
Florida (29)	49.1%	47.7%	1.4 %	2.2$	3.2 %
Pennsylvania (20)	48.8%	47.7%	1.1 %	2.4%	3.5 %
Michigan (16)	47.6%	47.3%	0.3 %	3.6%	5.1 %
Wisconsin (10)	47.9%	46.9%	1.0 %	3.6%	5.2 %

The numbers showed how history could have changed (assuming numbers are right); if 102722 votes changed hands, history would be different. The three states – PA, MI, and WA. Trump would have lost. Now in 2020, who are the third-party candidates? Can the Birthday party candidate make a difference? Let's see.

First thing first, Kayne West is the Birthday Party candidate. And we have Jo Jorgensen, the Libertarian Party candidate who has access to all 538 electoral votes. The Green Party candidate does not access to all electoral votes, but it is above 270. Can they and the other 16+ candidates make a difference? A one percent movement, either way, can make a big difference. What I believe will happen is that the coverage of the 3rd party candidate will be limited. And with the ongoing Pandemic, public movement and meeting the public will be limited. If I assume that 50% of the votes happened as the voter did not believe in Hillary or Trump. Now, these two percents are convinced to vote for Trump or against Trump. That will make a difference in a close election.

And as I write, I hear that Pennsylvania courts have removed the Green Party candidate. Last time the Party got 0.8% vote share or 48,912 votes. So what I wrote in the above paragraph is becoming right on the urban legend part. Do read the story of Dick Gregory, a comedian and African American who ran and could have potentially got Nine million votes, but something happened.

On analysis is that the key seems to be True. But I would like to keep it False due to the factors mentioned above. The Republicans need to come out in numbers and bring those who lean towards them to vote for President Trump. Here is where African American and Hispanic voters are going to make a difference to the swing states. More on that in the Battleground Chapter later.

Allan Lichtman Rating: True | **Clark Rating:** True

President Trump *Active Keys*: 3 vs. 3.5 (3 + 0 + 0.5)

Key #5
Short-Term Economy

*The economy during the election season is
Not in recession.*

Allan Lichtman Rating: False
*"The [coronavirus] pandemic has pushed the
economy into recession."*

The China virus, as President Trump calls it, has thrown a spanner to the wheels of economic transformation been carried out by him. Trump's goal was to generate jobs, increase disposable income across different communities, and bring in continuing economic growth in the underserved regions in the United States. The US is a service-driven economy that has been hit hard. An economy needs to be balanced – Agricultural to protect the national food supply, Industry (Mining and Manufacturing) to get critical things produced (for example, Steel, Medical supplies, Pharma drugs), and Services. United States GDP composition is service dominated. It is broken like the following:

Economic Sector GDP	2000	2017	Change
Service	72.82%	77.37%	~ 6%
Agriculture	1.15%	0.92%	~ -20%
Industrial	22.45%	18.21%	~ 19%+

The skew needs to be changed to create a balance. And President Trump is determined to do it. The United States has lost hundreds and thousands of manufacturing jobs, which has been outsourced. This happened at a higher pace over the last two decades with an increase in globalization and currency manipulation (what if all currency is pegged 1:1 or US$ value changes?). This will be a game-changer.

Since 2017 manufacturing jobs are rising. Many companies are making plans to set up or restart manufacturing in the United States.

The changing economic structure has hit a speed breaker. But once the Pandemic subsides, this change will continue. This realignment is necessary again for critical manufacturing needs. With the Pandemic in motion, the supply chain was hit. This needs to be also realigned. Another hit to the short-term economy is small business. With 99.9% of US businesses being small businesses accounting for close to 1.5 million new jobs every here, this business section is critical to providing a growth engine of nature. Some studies show 33% or one-third of the companies may never recover. These need to be rebuilt*.

These factors and determination of President Term will ensure jobs will be back in the United States in higher numbers, and new jobs will be created in new industries like technology. One sector which is needed to drive any of these economies sub-part is Technology. This is where the US will develop new avenues to boost the economy. Regarding the recession, Trump's policies (economic) kept the recession at bay for some time. But it would have hit sooner or later due to Federal Reserve policies of the last two decades. This is another point of discussion. For now, I will keep this rating as False.

In Key 7, you will see how small businesses' confidence is still high for President Trump.

Allan Lichtman Rating: False | **Clark Rating:** False

President Trump *Active Keys*: 3 vs. 3.5 (3 + 0 + 0.5)

Key #6
Long-Term Economy

Real annual per-capita economic growth during the term equals or exceeds mean growth during the two previous terms.

Allan Lichtman Rating: False
""The Pandemic has caused such negative GDP growth in 2020 that the key has turned false."

This is a tricky one. According to the definition, an incumbent will have a False rating in this key if the Real annual per-capita economic growth during the term equals or exceeds mean growth during the two previous terms. OK, so it means Obama years vs. Trump years. When I look at data, Obama years – 2009 to 2016 (first and second terms) shows an average value of $50,740 for GDP per capita. This, when taken in growth percentage terms, it is annualized to 0.68% growth, also taking into account the negative growth between 2008 to 2009. When the same details are checked for Trump's office period, the numbers looked great until the pandemic hits. And then it fell based on estimates currently coming. Let us see the table below.

	Obama (2009-2016)	Obama (2013-2016)	Trump (2017-2019)
Annual U.S. Real GDP Per Capita Since 1947 in 2012 Dollars	$50,740	$53,165	$56,587
GDP Growth average	0.69 %	1.43%	1.95%

Wow. Without the Pandemic, Trump's administration first three years is scoring above two terms or even the last term of Obama's administration. This shows some of the steps taken by Trump's administration. Another big area in which Trump's administration worked to create jobs in manufacturing. President Obama once said that the jobs are gone, and it is a new economy. It is (was) true. The US has been losing manufacturing jobs by the hundreds of thousands. The country lost 430,000 jobs during the Clinton Presidency final three years, and this continued during Bush year also. In eight years of Obama's

Presidency, around 300,000 manufacturing jobs were lost. Some estimates calculate that more than 91,000 plants with 5 million manufacturing jobs have been lost since 1998. In 2009 there was an essay from Robert B. Reich, former U.S. Secretary of Labor, "Manufacturing Jobs Are Never Coming Back." This is where the United States was. Donald Trump wanted to change this.

Since January 2017, when Donald Trump became the President, more than 480,000 manufacturing jobs had been added. When we compare the first 27 months of President Trump's term and the last 27 months of President Obama, the following chart showed the change.

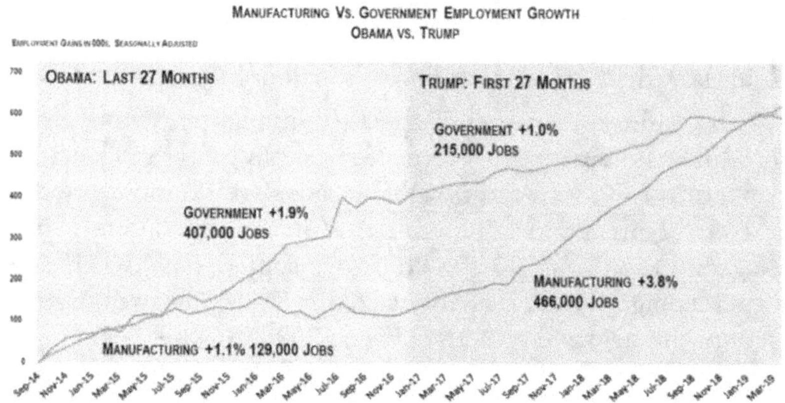

When the first 30 months are seen, then 314,000 manufacturing jobs were added. The top three states with manufacturing job growth were Nevada with 32.9%, Wyoming, 12.0%, and South Dakota, 10.0%.

So is the Key going to be false due to the Pandemic? Is the definition for Long Term Economy is right? Will no.

One subtle detail has been done differently now, which was not done to such an extent in previous recessions—a fiscal stimulus directly to the people and citizens of the United States. Yes, I believe millions of Americans receiving stimulus checks as high at $1,200 per individual with (with $500 per additional child) will be a game-changer. Stimulus checks were used in 2008, but not to the extent of what is done now in 2020. This check was part of a $2.2 trillion economic relief bill. And there are still talks of second stimulus checks coming in (at the time of writing this book). What did the citizens do with the currency given? Most said they saved or paid down debts. Studies showed that only around 40 percent of the total transfer was spent.

As you can see, this, along with the unemployment benefits, will keep a sort of lid of anger against this administration. Why? Because there is the help provided and plus a narrative been shared and talked about the slowdown. The slowdown is due to Coronavirus, and President Trump uses another term for it based on geography. This definitely is a way to distance oneself from the crashing economy as it has been deflected to China. The current economic situation and slowdown due to the Pandemic is not President Trump's fault. And if the message is spread and understood by the citizens, then this Key of Long-Term Economy will not be against him. There will be certain voters against him due to economic fallout. Still, as people begin to see the big picture – that he has shown enough examples that he is for broad economic prosperity, they will give Trump a thumbs up. When we need to see what Trump has done for the economy, we need to see who has been impacted. There are three broad categories I can place them based on what I know and read till now. These are Individual, Small Business, and Community. More on these in the next key around policies.

Another point to add is the change in wage growth across the United States for different communities and groups. In 2019, wages at all deciles of the black wage distribution exceeded earlier levels (2000 and 2007). Over the last 19 years, the Hispanic–white wage gap has reduced. From 12.3% in 2000, it was 10.8% in 2019. A jump was seen in 2019 compared to earlier years. This will be remembered. There was more disposable income in hands for households. Even if the negative narratives are run by certain mainstream media groups and Democrats (for gas lighting), these memories of disposable income increase will be remembered. There will be doubt, but not all may switch Trump off the radar. More have moved towards him, and few will go away. But there can be a net positive on the number of voters moving towards the Republic candidate.

Allan Lichtman Rating: False | **Clark Rating:** True (BIG ONE)

President Trump *Active Keys*: <u>3 vs. 4.5 (3 + 1 + 1.5)</u>

Key #7
Policy Change

The incumbent causes major changes in national policy.

Allan Lichtman Rating: True
"Through his tax cut, but mostly through his executive orders, Trump has fundamentally changed the policies of the Obama era."

America's declaration of independence genesis happened due to many factors. The incident I remembered studying was of an incident in Boston. Boston Tea Party is something I read in my eight standards in school. As years progressed, read more about the American Independence Movement and the Founding Fathers. One of the formative reasons for the revolution was various unpopular policies and (unjust) taxes. Taxation was done by a King on its colonies. Tea and taxes do not bode well. The fact is (unjust) taxes, especially on income, does not bode well. What the Trump 1.0 administration aimed for in this period was trying to undo policy restrictions that impact growth and provide more individual choices. There was a large number of decisions and orders carried out. As of October 1st (Hunters become the Hunted), the number of executive decisions looked like: (numbers are close)

- Executive Orders: 187
- Presidential proclamations: 515
- Other Presidential Documents: 299

Those are a lot of numbers. President Trump has also given a taste of liberty to taxpayers' earners by taking out the payroll tax. Imagine (to those whose income is taxed at the employee level), that there is no tax cut. It shows ZERO. A month before, the tax could have been multiple digits but now zero. Yes, it is possible. A cut in corporate tax rates with regulation changes to encourage small businesses was the right way ahead. The whole plan to promote job growth. Place down the seeds for "Made In America."

From my limited perspective of what I could see, hear, and read, I see a pattern. The pattern centered around business and individuals. The essence for most was around three zones. These are Individual, Small Business and Community, and Nation. Let us look into some:

1. **Individual & Family**: Tax Cuts, the most significant overhaul to tax code in over three decades. There were other benefits given. As per Census Bureau Current Population Survey data, middle-class incomes (adjusting for inflation) have surged by $5,003 since DJT became President in January 2017. (Oct 2019 period data). This makes an impact on saving, living, and investing for the future. True inflation has come, but think if that increase did not happen, then what?

2. **Small Business**: As more small businesses grew, more opportunities, more local employment, and increased middle class. According to a quarterly survey (Q1 2020) from CNBC and SurveyMonkey with small business owners, 64% of them approved of President Trump. This was on track till the Pandemic hit. But see the table below where the question was asked – "Do you approve or disapprove of the way Donald Trump is handling his job as president?"

	Q2 2017	Q2 2018	Q2 2019	Q1 2020	Q2 2020	Q3 2020
Net Approve	58%	59%	57%	64%	58%	59%
Strongly Approve	36%	36%	39%	**47%**	41%	41%
Strongly Disapprove	31%	32%	33%	29%	33%	34%

It is +5 points since he began his terms in strongly approve. And a +3 in strongly disprove. So a net +2 in terms of higher for strongly approve. Why is this important? Well, there are 30.7 million small businesses (less than 500 employees) in the United States. This compromise of 99.9% of all US businesses. Many have shut down in this Pandemic, and more can face issues. But based on the response, there is a high confidence level that his policies and the charisma he holds will bring him more votes in this period.

Another point is the continuity of the business. Yes, things are hit, but people do believe President Trump will get it back. He has the magic wand President Obama.

3. **Community**: First Step act; Opportunity zones, Manufacturing jobs, Outsourcing Jobs act
4. **Nation**: Space Force, larger defense budgets with new programs, healthcare reforms, lower drug prices, usage of Defense Production Act, Border Wall, and more

There were more policies that I cannot cover here, but there had been a lot of coordinated effort. The impact of these policies and the narrative and messaging of these policies will have a more considerable influence not only in the nation but also in the swing states.

Note:

The Defense Production Act: This act of 1950 was used by Trump during the current pandemic period. It was essential to allow civil enterprises to be part of a broader nation's defense against the virus. US corporates got into action and developed critical supplies needed for the country. In the future, all nations will think of their critical need's products (like Steel and Medical supplies).

Allan Lichtman Rating: True | **Clark Rating:** True (BIG ONE)

President Trump *Active Keys*: <u>4 vs. 5.5 (4 + 1 + 0.5)</u>

Key #8
Social Unrest

There is no sustained social unrest during the campaign.

Allan Lichtman Rating: False
"There has been considerable social unrest on the streets, with enough violence to threaten the social order."

What is the definition of social unrest? When I started looking at various definitions, it had certain things in common – a section of the population does not like something happening. They create unrest and change may or may not occur. So, we have a Group, an Issue, Modus of Action, and a Result. Some examples of social unrest below

Theme	What Is It?	Example
Political	Citizen comes to the street against the government system or ruling	Arab Spring Color Revolution (we will visit this later in the book)
Variations in international commodity prices	Increase prices, shortage of commodity, food price increases	Venezuela
Economic shocks	The economy of a nation tanks	Soviet Union Fall, Venezuela, Argentina
Racial and Ethnic Tensions	Slaughter of fellow citizens due to difference in ethnicity or race	Rwanda
Unrest can also be from Droughts, Rainfall Shocks, and environment		

When I think of social unrest in the US in the past, I think of: 1960s: Civil Movement; 1970s: Vietnam War Demonstration; 1980s: Miami riots (Police killing) and others; 1990s: Rodney King riots, Woodstock incident, others; 2000s: BART police shooting and other few protests; 2010s: Occupy Wall Street and others.

In the current 2020 period, there are protests which are centered around racial tensions. The BLM (Black Life Matter) protests were ongoing. The death of George Floyd acted as a catalyst for the protests to spread across different parts of the United States. These emotionally-charged protests will have an impact on how voters will vote. But there were also certain protests which went violent, leading to arson, burning down and even attack police officers. The narrative is now diverging towards two different streams—how much and what kinds of protests are acceptable to a voter's mind. The Pandemic impacted the lives of many, with small businesses hit hard. With arson, looting of shops, and attack on the police, it becomes a law and order issue for the government on the ground and voters' minds. So, the question is to note the impact of these arsons and quantum of spread. Based on the time writing this book, they were cities like Portland, Chicago, St Louis (and others) where news of protests getting out of control. In some of these areas, there were cases of arson and looting. Notice anything in common. These locations have Mayors, District Attorney, Congressional majority, Governors, Senators who are all Democrats. With the protests and particular left inspired mob violence, life and small business has been hit. I saw a video of African American female crying to not destroy their living as that is all they have. But what I see an American citizen appealing to fellow Americans to please help her not ruin her livelihood. Or Civilians who were not part of protests died also. Like a case of 77 years old retired police Captain who was shot trying to protect his friend's pawnshop. His death was live-streamed on Facebook at 2.30 am. Even in the Democrat-dominated New York has hundreds of shops boarded up to protect from riots. Why? Why is this necessary? Can we learn anything from history?

I started going through history to see if they were examples of race riots in the United States. I came across Red Summary Riots. The more I read about this, I noticed that the recent events were not like the race riots earlier a hundred years ago. The Red Summer riots, which happened in 1915-20, was run by White Supremacist. That was a different United States. The 60s had the civil rights movement bringing in much-needed changes. The United States has always moved forward. We need to remember the past. If not discussed, we tend to repeat it.

With the rise of social media and more medium of exchange, yes, there is more amplification of the noise. But it is now not only about noise quality but also what is the counter-narrative. There is a quick resolution where the broader picture is shared, and the full context comes in. It is a thin line where mainstream media channels can provide a narrative needed to suit their agenda. But the American way of life is about Liberty. And it is this liberty the citizens will protect and share a counter-narrative of the (not-so) perceived truth.

Over many months in the last two years, there are stories of walk-away movement where old democrat voters walk away from the Democrat party. There was also a fabulous campaign ad for House elections MD-7 by Republican Congressional Nominee Kimberly Klacik. This campaign advert showed how Baltimore has been hit over the last many decades across various social indicators and life metrics. And it is not only Baltimore. The decreasing quality of life is across many Democratic-run cities. See the Top-ranked cities in violent crime per 100,000 people per year

#	Violent Crime	Democratic / Socialist Mayor Since	Murder and Nonnegligent manslaughter	Democratic/ Socialist Mayor Since
1	St. Louis	1949	St. Louis	1949
2	Detroit	1962	Baltimore	1967
3	Baltimore	1967	Detroit	1962
4	Memphis	1967	New Orleans	1873
5	Kansas City	1991	Baton Rouge	2005
6	Milwaukee	1908	Kansas City	1991
7	Cleveland	1989	Cleveland	1989

These top ten cities of violent crime are X% of the US population. It has been under Democratic governorship, and even Mayors and DA when we look into each detail with a toothcomb. The question is why people keep electing the same. Is it the population that has been gaslighted? Or is it mass hypnosis? Or is it our emotional buttons are being pressed and manipulated to not think logically.

As human beings, we are tuned to help each other. We cooperated, we socialize, and lend a hand. This is a natural way. But when social unrest is targeted at bystanders, an ordinary person gets impacted. This is not normal. This is what has been seen across the United States now. This is not normal. The filter of freedom and liberty will be switched on. People will rise above prejudice and vote for Trump and the Republican party. The party of law and order.

So, my analysis is that the key is True in favor of Trump. Through the narrative, Americans will see that they have been pushed and understand that all need to rise together and preserve the US value of Freedom and Liberty. They will do it for the love of their country.

Allan Lichtman Rating: False | **Clark Rating:** (?)

President Trump *Active Keys*: 4 vs. 6 (4 + 1 + 1)

Key #9
Scandal

The incumbent administration is untainted by major scandals.

Allan Lichtman Rating: False
""As I predicted, Trump was impeached. Plus, he has plenty of other scandals."

Quick question. When does scandal make an impact? When is it sudden and unusual? Or when it is another one in a long list which does not stop? President Trump's last five years, from Candidate Trump to President Trump to now incumbent Trump, has been a rollercoaster ride. There was one scandal after another, according to mainstream media. Everything he did, said, and even though was dissected and discussed. What happened in the end? Nothing. The stickiness of the scandal did not tarnish his image towards his core supporters. But did it impact the Democrat voters or Independent voters? My analysis is not so much. Many stuck in their positions and already formed opinions. What needs to be seen is what is the narrative President Trump is speaking about. He is speaking on action and activities done. That is something that he will remind the different voters. He will remind on the issues the voters care about. I will speak about this more later in chapter Battleground. For now, lets us see how this scandal key is not False but neutral or true.

A sample list of scandals or negative narrative stories ran against President Trump over the last four years.
1. 2017: Russia-Russia | Very Fine People
2. 2018: Mueller's Russia | Mental Fitness
3. 2019: Whistle Blower | Impeachment
4. 2020: On& On (Do I need to fill? Media has no other job)

When we list of these scandals reported by the media, then it becomes like A...B...C...D........R for Russia.... W for Whistle Blower. Get it. It is a long list, and anything and everything is wrong. Some reports mention that Donald Trump gets 95% negative press coverage. How and why? With such coverage, his administration power should have paralyzed, and things should not have been moving ahead. But it did till the pandemic. And the recovery is underway. So with all these scandals, will this impact the Presidential election. Let us see a bit from the past on how scandals impacted the race. And when I say scandal, I mean the one that sticks and changes the voter's mind. Please note I am only considering the Presidential years. And we can see the scandal does not stop. But will it impact elections as it did before? Let's look at the past Presidential scandals in the last fifty years. These scandals were part of discourse not only in US politics but also around the world. And it is something for the history books. These were:

- Watergate: Nixon (he stepped down)
- Monica Lewinsky: Bill Clinton (Al Gore was impacted as it was a close election)

Both of these scandals did not impact the incumbent both did not seek reelection. Which scandals make an impact in mind? I leave the judgment to you. But what the mainstream media and left-aligned channels and media have done is that overused this card. Scandals make an impact when it hits the subconscious mind. When this happens, it changes the perception filter around the candidate, especially for those in the middle, and not deciding who they will vote for. The way the media had run narratives over the last two decades and the changing social dynamics have led to a polarized world. Even in the US, I remember seeing an image that showed the centralist has reduced, and citizens have moved either towards left progressive liberal or conservative values. This means of these terms have changed over many years. I will not be discussing this here but will say that most citizens have already decided who they will vote for, no matter what. No matter what?

Well, for any scandal to make an impact now, it will need to be gigantic. Not only that, but it must also be a soul-wrenching one. Something which can impact within an individual, cohort, or group moral compass. And these are the words – 'moral' and 'compass.' With changing times, what issues are ethical in one eye has changed, and it does not move the dial enough to change the voting pattern. The mainstream media and the virtual world have drowned us in Anti-Trump narratives for the last four years in such a way that the tolerance level has increased. The issue is that these narratives and scandals have not stuck to President Trump. There were counter-narratives, and these issues (or scandals) were found to be wrong and biased without the complete picture been shown, or context is given. Yes, I will be attacked for such statements. Still, studies showing the anti-Trump bias shown are never seen before against any President in US history. Project Veritas spy cams show some of these. One can go to their website, see it with their own eyes, hear with their own ears, and think and connect with their own brains.

Scandals need to stick and change the views of voters. When the media is scoring low on credibility, their news around the scandals are not useful in gas-lighting or switching off the voters. With the soaring popularity of President Trump among the base has made him an unsinkable ship. The ship will move ahead now.

So, my analysis is that the key is almost True in favor of Trump. There is still an October surprise or surprises which can come. But it seems both sides will have surprises to deal with. A narrative and counter-narrative and vice-versa. Net-Net the impact may be neutral or skewed towards President Trump. The key is in active play, so a 0.5 for me.

Allan Lichtman Rating: False | **Clark Rating:** (?)

President Trump *Active Keys*: 4 vs. 6.5 (4 + 1 + 1.5)

Key #10
Foreign or Military Failure

The incumbent administration suffers no major failure in foreign or military affairs.

Allan Lichtman Rating: True
*"We've had some very difficult moments with Donald Trump,
but so far, true."*

Yes. This is one point which I agree with 100%. Yes, they were difficult moments. But in his own unique way, things were handled, and no military or diplomatic failure has occurred. This is because the number of successes has been many. That I will list and share my views in the next key. For now, when I look at near-failures, it is something that cannot be revisited. For example, President Trump could not get a nuclear deal with North Korea. But there was no hostile reaction towards the United States by the North Korean government. Like that, they were many other areas where they were challenges, but no failures came in a big way. Instead, there have been successes. And such success will be written by historians that this was the moment when things turned for the better in many regions. Let us explore some of them in the next key. For now, this is True.

Allan Lichtman Rating/CALL: True | **My Rating:** True

President Trump *Active Keys*: 5 vs. 7.5 (5 + 1 + 1.5)

Key #11
Foreign or Military Success

The incumbent administration achieves a major success in foreign or military affairs.

Allan Lichtman Rating: False
"While Trump hasn't had any big, splashy failures, he hasn't had any major successes either."

Boom, BOOM, BOOM! What are these BOOMS? These are sounds of success of President Trump and his administration on Foreign policy and Military action. The fact is there are multiple booms and not three. But I will group these booms into three big BOOMS. These are Peace, Trade, and Security. Let us visit them.

- **Peace:** Here, I define peace as relevant to the United States and those regions of the world where its interest lies.
- **Middle East:** The peace deal in September between Israel – UAE, and Bahrain is not a one-off deal for the show. Saudi Arabia will follow to normalize its relationship with Israel soon. By allowing a commercial Israel airline to fly over the Kingdom of Saudi Arabia, airspace is the first step. Plus, Prince M.B.S is a strong partner for Trump. The Abraham Accords Peace Agreement, as it is called, will be the starting step for the death knell for terrorism from both sides. The economy will gain a boost due to trade between the different countries. The name selected also had a lot of deep meaning. Abraham is seen as the father of the Arab people and the Jewish people through his two sons. This is a start. As President Trump has said, there will be peace in the Middle East. Once he wins the election again, Iran will fall in line. For India. Will Pakistan change its tune?
- **North Korea:** President Trump accepted North Korea's leader Kim's Invitation and met him on Jun 12, 2018, in Singapore. It was a great diplomacy show. And his meeting on the border (DMZ) of North and South Korea on June 30th, 2019, at 38 Parallel north showed bonhomie between the two leaders. President Trump becomes the first sitting US President to set foot in North Korea.

This was a different approach. Yes, it is true the Vietnam summit a few months back in February 2019 failed. But it is a step. President Trump walked away as he did not want to give a lot of concessions. Message received. The North Koreans now had to face a US President who asked for things to be done and changed. The impact. Well, there is still no mushroom clouds. Many said North Korea will fire missiles at the United States or its allies and start the war. We are a four-year clock now. What happened? NOTHING!
Coming back to the Vietnam summit, no deal was signed between the United States and North Korea, but it is a step forward. As I heard someone say - from confrontation to cooperation. In the second term, the deal will be signed.

- **Trade**: From Globalization to America First. The steps taking by the President is not only about jobs, but also about national security. Or like I would like to say, about Continuity of (Independent) Living.

    - **Multi-Country Trade Agreement**: There were trade deals not convenient to the US. For example, NAFTA is being replaced by USMCA (United States–Mexico–Canada Agreement). The Trans-Pacific Partnership (TPP) was revoked. The President has shown intent on keeping America First. United States of America is still part of WTO, but this may change with a second term.

    - **Tariffs**: The sea of Tariffs done by President Trump has the America First factor in it. Tariffs were placed on various products like Steel Production and countries like China and Mexico, among others. The Tariffs done have provided an advantage to the United States. Many companies have decided and made moves to come back or increase manufacturing back in the United States. Not everything worked, but making companies think in this direction is the first sign of change in the business model's structure. From my point of view, Tariffs helps against currency devaluation advantage taken by certain countries. The impact will be positive in the long term only if it is done in a structured way. With the supply chain question around China as a manufacturing base, it has been seen that Trump was right all along. The lack of capacity for critical products showed an underbelly of danger on the nation's need. President Trump then used a trump card, the **Defense**

Production Act (which I have elaborated earlier). America first will lead to the Nation first. But every country's culture and nation are important, and one can work together. Trump has emphasized this in his UN speech.

- **Trade Deals**: Various trade deals were signed across the planet. Some of it was beneficial to the USA, and some did not get the desired results. Like President Trump came to India and all likelihood there were talks that a trade deal, a golden standard trade deal, would be signed. But it did not come up with President Trump saying India Prime Minister is a tough negotiator. Was it possible that the deal was done, but the news about GOLD changed it? On Feb 22nd, an announcement was made of a massive discovery of gold mines in India. It was said 3,000 tones of gold were found. After about twenty-four hours of news coverage, it was told there was no gold, but a calculation error was there. First, this announcement was made by a government department. It was done just x days before President Trump landed in India. Third, why wait for so long before sharing the news that there is no gold of that amount. Is it related to getting a better Trade Deal (from India's perspective)? Not sure. Just speculation here. Time will tell. But President Trump did secure trade deal with other nations. This is an ongoing battle of the nations. When he wins the elections in 2020, then there will be more deals done in 2021.

Is President Trump against the multi-trade agreement?

No, he is not. The deals should be a win-win and be with likeminded countries – something like Democracies of value. I foresee that QUAD – Quadrilateral Security Dialogue, an informal forum for security, evolves into a trade partnership. The countries in QUAD – Japan, Australia, India, and the United States. It will have countries like the UK in the future and more. Watch this space to develop. Overall, success in this section is mixed and neutral but not negative. In the long term, it will help protect the US way of living. Liberty and Freedom.

- **Security**: This section is around United States security and global security to the free world.

- **ISIS**: When I think of ISIS, two things come to my mind. First, from where the 'HELL' did it come and get the base to grow. Imagine - weapons, people, supply chain, clearance, and freedom to operate. And second, Nobel Peace Prize-winning President Obama saying

ISIS is something which will continue for ten years or more. Something which the world needs to prepare for the long run. Really! Nazi Germany, with all its operating machinery, could be defeated in under four years (considering when Allies went into offensive – 1941-45). And here we have the President and Leader of the Free World speaking that ISIS cannot be defeated. So, what happened. Well, President Trump (they thought she could not loose) happened. On October 26, 2019, when Al-Baghdadi was being chased by US Special Forces, he must be thinking how the tables have been turned from support to chase. The good boy came into the limelight here. The next successor of ISIS was also killed. From thousands of miles of calling it a caliphate to hiding in a cave and finally dying alone and cold. That is what happens when responsible action is taken.

- **Iran:** The United States canceled the Joint Comprehensive Plan of Action (JCPOA) with Iran. The 2015 agreement on Iran's nuclear program had a lot of concession

  The drone Strike on Qasem Soleimani and his death was one bold move shown by President Trump. The United States is not afraid to act. A potential Deep State asset, Soleimani was responsible for US and allied servicemen and civilians' deaths. His death ensures that his followers will think ten times before acting against the free world. Many Iranian who have taken up citizenship of another nation welcomed the move. They know the local story in Tehran.

- **Recognizing Jerusalem:** In December 2017, President Trump administration recognized Jerusalem as the Capital of Israel. The embassy moved (just like in London).

These are some of the successes. And remember. Always remember, there has been no NEW WAR. This is true for me.

Allan Lichtman Rating: False | **Clark Rating:** True

President Trump *Active Keys*: 5 vs. 8.5 (5 + 2 + 1.5)

Key #12
Incumbent Charisma

The incumbent party candidate is charismatic

Allan Lichtman Rating: False
"Trump is a great showman, but he only appeals to a narrow slice of Americans."

Personal charm. Attractiveness. Captivating. These are some of the words which come in my mind when I think of Charisma. What kind of charm or magic can an individual weave around a group of people of different backgrounds? The United States is a melting pot of different cultures, races, ethnicity, thinking. A diverse, rich country where citizens can keep multiple identifies but believe in freedom and liberty. To reach out to such a wide range of souls would need the ultimate charmer. Richard J. Wiseman, a Professor of the Public Understanding of Psychology, views a charismatic person. According to him, such persons are highly attuned to the emotions of others. Not only that, such a person can increase the emotion level in others while keeping one's feelings in check. Many come to the mind. But is Donald Trump such a charmer? Let's explore.

When I first came to know about Trump was in the 90s while in college, studying in Mangalore, India. Mangalore is 13,237 km or 8,225 miles from New York City. It was a copy of the book 'The Art of The Deal,' in a local bookstore. I picked, seeing the smiling face on the cover. There was something about the cover page and the title of the book. I scanned through the pages and read a few passages. Interesting. I picked it up, and over the next ten years, I picked and read other books by him. With the advent of the internet in the late 90s, I also searched for Donald Trump. It was a different time as the pages came up slowly. For me, his words, positivity, straight messaging I got hooked on. I did not watch most of his shows on TV. Just caught it here and there but did see him give interviews and talks. He had a magnetism. And thought process. He loved his country and the people around him. He is a PATRIOT. Many spoke about the good he did. He was on various talk shows. Like Ophrah. Now, will Ophrah get a racist to her show? And that is something I never got. When did Trump become a racist? He even won an award given to those who supported African American communities. The more you search, hear, and talk, the more you think the question – why is such a picture been painted for Trump? Is there an agenda? So coming back, does he have charisma? The answer is Yes.

One thing Trump is good at is that the is tuned to with culture. He understands how thinking and culture, especially social culture, is changing with different generation and knows how to communicate. Micro messaging is what he knows, and does that regular. I will share more details in the Battleground chapter, which is ahead. According to Pew Research, 38% of individuals identify as political independents with a 13% skewing towards republicans and 17% leaning towards democrats. This truly leaves 7% who are centralists. For any political candidate charisma to work, it must significantly impact this 38% to win the elections. This is where a motivated base who reach out through different channels come into play. Suppose the political leader has a strong charisma. In that case, they can then push their base to reach out, talk to those leaning or in the center, and those across the other side to listen and understand their point of view. This is where Trump first, and now President Trump's charisma will work. To bring in more citizens into his fold to vote for America. To vote for their country's future. Just search the #WalkAway Movement and see Liberals and Democrats walk away from the current Democratic party. Certain African Americans say the Democrats want to keep them in the plantation of guilt and not allow them to rise up. And when they speak up, the current Democratic nominee Biden says if you are not black, you don't vote for them. Sheesh!

Well, in short. Leaders draw supporters with charisma. Supporters get passionate enough to bring more into their fold.

Allan Lichtman Rating: False | **Clark Rating:** True

President Trump *Active Keys*: <u>5 vs. 9.5 (5 + 3 + 1.5)</u>

Key #13
Challenger Charisma

The challenging party candidate is not charismatic.

Allan Lichtman Rating: True
""Biden is a decent, empathetic person, but he's not inspirational or charismatic."

Yes! End of story?

Well, Biden is not charismatic. He does not have charisma. He is giving questions to people on what to ask.

Biden, if he drops out and Harris takes over, she also has no charisma. During the Democratic Primaries, she garnered less than 3% of the votes, which shows how she resonated with her principals and charisma. And if there is a new candidate (O?), which is for energizing the base, then the same result. Lack of charisma.

The Democratic party has now had Trump Derangement Syndrome for over four years and will have another four. At the end, who knows, the Democratic party may not exist, and it is broken up. This has happened before. Check the United States presidential election of 1800. There were two parties, which does not exist anymore - the Democratic-Republican party and Federalist. Or the Whig party of the 19th century. Twice the Whig party was in control of the House – in 1841-43 and 1847-49 and had three Presidents. They were the 10th, 12th, and 13th President of the United States.

Who knows… Democratic party will change, evolve, or go down in history? Time will tell. But what if Michele Obama or Oprah or anyone else come into play in this election if Biden steps down?

Allan Lichtman Rating: True | **Clark Rating:** True

President Trump *Active Keys*: <u>6 vs. 10.5 (6 + 3 + 1.5)</u>

Conclusion to the Keys

Nine (9) keys are active (True) in play for me. And another three keys are going to be influential, which will play True in some Battleground states. For Allan Lichtman, there are only 6 (six) keys are active. What if he gets it wrong? Well, he has made ready a caveat. According to him, the only scenario his 32 years of accuracy in forecasting will fail due to election meddling, foreign interference, or voter suppression. No, not again. What is this been talked about? Is it a way to set up a ground for Russia, Russia, Russia again? Or mail in ballots confusion, which will rise and questions which have been raised. Facebook and other tech giants also saying the election are not over during election day. But I believe Patriots are in Control, and we will see the truth soon. For now, lets us think about what Trump's action needs to do for the future.

There was a movie in India with the name *Roti Kapda aur Makaan* (1974), which comes to mind when I think of what President Trump has done. When we translate the words literally, it is Bread, Cloth, and House. The movie title core meaning meant that the people need these three things to survive – Food, Clothing, and Shelter. When I look at the keys and what President Trump has done, it moves towards securing these things for the United States citizens. I see the keys in the following ways:

- Food: Increase the ability to earn, save and grow
- Clothing: Protect a way of life – Liberty, and Freedom
- Shelter: Enhance security, internal and external, social equity

These policies drive towards freedom of thinking and speaking. One may pick points here and there, but I feel policies are directly or indirectly impacts the factors I have highlighted above. President Trump is not trying to win big battles always. But small steps and activities will have a multiplier effect. I deal with this in Chapters 8 and 9. For now, let us see the keys if seen not as pure binary but as a 2X2 matrix.

One axis is around the Key categories – True or False. The measure is a negative impact on the positive impact. So, if the key is more to the right end of the chart, it is positive. If a particular key is towards the left, it is a more negative measure for the current Trump administration.

President Trump *Active Keys*: <u>6 vs. 10.5 (6 + 3 + 1.5)</u>

CHAPTER 6
Soothsayers 2020 | Tippy Top

Who can see the future? There were druids to see the vision, astrologers to see the stars, or palmist to see the hands. Now we have a new range of soothsayers in the political prediction field. As I would like to call them, these soothsayers, Statidatastics Priests, have their rules and magical chants. These Statidatastics Priests are placing using science, math, and technology to develop the results they call out. They use a set of rules they understand and develop it further towards a conclusion. All these conclusions are in black and white with a hint of probability. In the table below are the forecasts given for the 2020 Presidential elections as of Oct 9-19

Name	Result
Cook Political Report Electoral College Forecast	Dem: 290 Rep: 163
Inside Elections Presidential Ratings	Dem: 319 Rep: 188
The Economist's US Presidential Election Forecast	Dem: 334 Rep: 164
PredictIt Market Probabilities	Dem: 334 Rep: 204
Politico 2020 Presidential Forecast	Dem: 268 Rep: 203
Princeton Election Consortium	Dem: 351 Rep: 149
JHK Forecasts Presidential Election Forecast	Dem: 348.5 Rep: 189.5
CNN 2020 Electoral College Map	Dem: 319 Rep: 188
U.S. News Electoral College Ratings	Dem: 290 Rep: 185

Yes, the Democratic party will win in a landslide in both Electoral College votes and popular votes. One poll that takes nine major polls sees the Democrat take 290 Electoral College seats and Republicans 163. The rest are tossups. The high is 348 seats for Dems, and our favorite CNN gives Biden a big victory with 319 seats. I really wonder why there is a need to have an election. You have the mainstream media and armchair experts deciding the decision.   What we need to understand is such results can be used as a narrative controller. In a world of psyops, data can be used for social engineering, and these Statidatastics Priests, along with Mainstream Media, can try to make new narratives. The question they need to answer is how they got it so wrong in 2016. If in 2020, Donald Trump wins the election — both seats and popular vote, then they need to really apologize to the world and look at what they are doing. And if President Trump wins BIG! I wonder what situation will then be. It will be a tippy-top shape for President Trump then. But there is one question in my mind.

One question for the professor and these priests, what happens if Biden drops off. Or there is a BIG October surprise.

Tippy Top: Speech Reference from President Trump

President Trump has used the word Tippy Top twice. Once during easter in 2018, when he said the White House is in Tippy Top shape, and the second time in Rush's show in October to describe the nuclear weapon as in Tippy Top shape. The soothsayer's predictions are not in tippy-top shape.

CHAPTER 7
October Surprise | Death Blossom

Presidential Elections and October Surprises go hand in hand in US elections. Why wouldn't it be, as Halloween is around the corner? In this period, the political atmosphere is charged and tense. As there is a strong history suggesting that skeletons in Presidential candidates' closets will be exposed during this time. Or something out of the ordinary happen which charges the tide of the election. The public of the United States, the media, and politics gurus worldwide are on the lookout for a so-called October surprise. In American political slang, the term October surprise refers to a perfectly timed news event that will get tons of media coverage, manipulate the public emotions and opinions, and perhaps will permanently change the course and outcome of the presidential elections. The US presidential elections always occur in early November; hence any such news event in late October greatly influences public minds and voters' opinions. As public opinion shifts, the election results are inevitably affected.

For 2016, the Trump Hollywood Access tapes, Hillary Clinton email scandal (which I think the email will resurface in 2020 also as it still not resolved – hint Winer's laptop). This year in 2020, the October month has begun. We have already seen the Supreme Court nomination Senate hearing coming up. President Trump was getting Covid-19, went to the hospital, and came back to the White House. What will happen this month is up to speculation, and I will share a few views on the coming page. First, let us look a bit of the past.

History of October Surprises:
The term was coined not so long ago by Casey William when serving as the campaign manager for Ronal Reagan's presidential campaign (1980's). But the phenomenon itself dates back a lot longer. There are several examples to look back on.

1972- Richard Nixon Vs. McGovern:
Republican President Richard Nixon was running for reelection in 1972. The Vietnam war was raging on despite the four long years of

negotiation. Senator George McGovern was running against him, with an antiwar manifesto. Just 12 days before the presidential elections, National Security Advisor Henry Kissinger held a press conference at the White House and declared the famous line 'We believe that peace is at hand.' Resultantly Nixon's popularity rose among the masses, and he outpolled McGovern in all the states except two. McGovern called this move 'a cruel political deception. For peace was most definitely not anywhere on the horizon at the time. It was no earlier than 1975 when the US military involvement in Vietnam was finally withdrawn.

1980- Carter Vs. Reagan:

In the presidential elections held in 1980, the hot issue was American hostages held in Iran. The then democratic president Carter was running for reelection. The Republican opposition based their campaign on highlighting that American citizens' continued captivity is proof of the American government's weakness under the democratic rule.

The October surprise came in Iran's denial to negotiate with the American govt while Carter was in the white house. On the 21st of October, the Iranian prime minister declared that the hostages would not be released. The situation naturally caused a sense of national malaise, fingers were pointed at Carter's leadership, and Reagan's competency took full advantage. Later it was revealed that certain operatives (George Bush was running as VP. He was ex-CIA chief. Hmmm.) had meetings with Iranian agents in Paris. They promised Iran arms for their war against Iraq if Iran pledged to delay the release of hostages until after the elections.

2006- Donald Trump Vs. Hillary Clinton:

In the 2016 presidential elections, there were two October surprises. On October 7, Donald Trump's Access Hollywood tape was released in which he was using explicit language and passing sexist remarks. Obviously, it did not sit well with several people. Several prominent politicians from both the parties expressed their disapproval, and some even asked him to step aside as a presidential candidate. Though Trump had been accused of sexist behavior and remarks before, he claimed that these remarks do not reflect who he is. These are the kind of blatantly audacious remarks people have come to expect of President Trump.

On the same memorable day of October 7, the famous Wikileaks began, several emails and excerpts were released from the account of

John Podesta. The leaks were around Hillary Clinton, included voice excerpts on different speeches given by Hillary Clinton on other occasions. These portrayed her stance on trade deals differently from what was purported by Clinton during her campaign. I remember CNN warning us not to see this public website as illegal, and there can be issues. But for them, it is legal. CNN actually said whatever needs to be learned from WikiLeaks needs to be heard from them. So much for fair media. In the last week of October, the pandora box of Hillary's emails was opened. Then FBI director James Comey announced in a letter sent to congress that there will be an investigation into the emails related to Hillary Clinton's use of a private email server. Comey's dubious and vague letter stated that the FBI had found new emails that might or might not be about the email scandal. Suspicious information released at such a critical time during the election campaign shook the voters. Even her staunch supporters were distracted by the portrayal of Hillary Clinton as a corrupt crook and traitor. Trump won the election; these leaks could have made an impact in states with close elections.

As for the server, will more news come out in 2020 with the Ukrainian Government speaking about bribes given by companies to Bidens? Moreover, there are stories that Democratic servers (so-called) hacked in the 2016 period are actually out there.

2020 Presidential Elections: Trump Vs. Biden (or Harris or O/D)

And now for the 2020 presidential elections, voters of the United States of America are holding their breaths for what October surprise will be brought forward this year. There are many speculations regarding Trumps' possible strategies for winning the presidential elections this year. Many may be in the offing.

- COVID Hero Card: Get a cure– therapeutics or vaccine.
- COVID Survivor: Trump has come back from the Hospital after getting infected with COVID. He recovers. He is a fighter and a survivor. Respect as a fighter. Share of the voice of Democrats and Biden goes down in the media as coverage is Trump.
- Foreign Policy – Troops coming back home: The campaign promise of no more needless wars is something Trump has kept. In fact, I don't remember when it was no US President started a war (at least from Regan onwards – 40 years). We might hear of the withdrawal of the troops, 26000 from Germany, 8000 from Afghanistan. On the

same note, there might be a partial or complete withdrawal of US troops currently in South Korea.

- Foreign Policy – Iran: Iran's nuclear program. Trump ordering an airstrike against Iran or going in a completely opposite direction might rejoin the JCPOA
- China: Tough action against China?
- Declassification of Intel Documents: The Declassification of Intel documents (Obama era); could show how they spied on his campaigns and, worse, his presidency (Deep State Coup).
- Biden Corruption: More details can be released of the tactics used by the old administration will come out
- Release of declassified documents (by mistake), many documents were released, showing the manipulation carried out against Trump.

Whatever the surprise, we will be hearing some of these terms soon

Crossfire Hurricane | Steele's dossier | DNC Server | Crowdstrike | Child Trafficking (#SaveOurChildren) | FISA | Supreme Court Vacancy | Gold Standard | Hillary Arrest | Silver Standard | Haiti Children | New Monetary System | CBDC – Central Bank Digital Currency | IMF-SDRs | End of US dollar (reserve currency) | 25th Amendment | QAnon or JFK (Jr) | Term Limit on House & Senate | Legislative Branch Audit on income | Biden Indicted & Stepping Down | Tulsi stepping in or O

Death Blossom: *Movie reference,* a scene in Star Fighter.

This is a prototype weapon. The idea is to let your enemies or adversaries come close to you, and then use this superweapon called Death Blossom. It can be used once only. And when used, every adversary in the range is decimated. It is the universe's most potent weapon. Is the October Surprise a set of news that will make fake media and their voices on social media to question not Donald Trump but everyone else? Time will tell.

CHAPTER 8
Citizens vs. Tribe | WWG1WGA

What builds a nation? Family and communities. There is a block of values in a family. And a group of families comes together to form communities. These various communities across multiple regions form a nation. The basic unit of a family is an individual educated by internal family dynamics, external environment of what one perceives and understands. In a diverse country like the United States, there is a diversity of cultures and thoughts. These thoughts need to be connected. There needs to be resonation leading to harmony.

The voters are humans. And humans are rational and irrational. There is a battle for our minds to decide. This is what the voters in the United States are facing. When I think how different cohort of the population who will make an impact in the election these are:

- Immigrants
- African Americans
- Hispanics
- US Armed Forces and Law Enforcement

Immigrants and Impact in Presidential Voting

The United States of America, a country built by immigrants, has been a destination for millions. Why? To live the American Dream. But what is the American Dream? For me, it is liberty, freedom of thought, and the rule of law. As a result, if I want to make big, I can do it with my strength of intellect and hard work (plus some luck on the way would not be bad). In short, there are opportunities for success and prosperity to raise social stature with few barriers. Many have made it big, and we have seen examples. This is what brings immigrants to the United States. Immigrants, both legal and illegal. For now, I limit my thoughts to legal immigrants.

There are over 45 million immigrants in the United States. In terms of numbers, it is the largest in the world for a country. These immigrants are working in the different institutions of the states and playing their role in the progress of the US economy. Close to 14% of the residents in the United States are born in a foreign country. Within this group, 50% of them are naturalized citizens. The largest number of foreign-born immigrants are from Mexico. They account for ~16% of all eligible immigrants. Then the Philippines, India, China, and Vietnam. Now think what kind of relationship Trump had with these countries. These actions will impact voters.

The matter of fact is that one seven US residents are an immigrant. What is needed is cohesive integration with the American Dream and allowing everyone to thrive and have the need to protect Freedom and Liberty. In 2016, Trump conducted the presidential election, his election objective and slogan were "Immigration concerns." The media thought illegal immigrants would be arrested and deported. But the interesting fact is in the tenure of Trump, the deporting immigrants are lesser than Obama.

With these facts, it is important to note that immigrants have a substantial impact on the elections. In 2020, the foreign-born immigrants who are voting can change a toss-up state. There are data to suggest there has been an increased registration of voters (legal residents) who are foreign-born. According to the Pew research report, 10% of eligible foreign voters in the presidential election of 2020 will be foreign-born citizens.

Political support of Immigrants in the USA

Political support of (many) immigrants can depend on how they perceive the relationship the United States have with their old country and how they see the future a political party or President can provide. Immigrants left their country and lived in another country for better opportunities, for a better lifestyle, business and job opportunities, freedom, peace, etc. Some surveys indicate that the split may be 50-50 support. So, what the Trump administration has done is spreading the message of his work. The things he was worked out with many countries and most, protection of the American Dream. If the immigrants have decided to be a United States citizen, it is because of opportunities. Not because of chance it can move towards socialism.

An example is where Trump's specific actions — for or against a country- can impact the voters. For example, voters who had their linkage to Iran need to see what Trump has done to Iran. For many, General Qasem Soleimani was a tormentor for many in Iran. Taking him out gave many Iranian Americans who in business, entrepreneurs, and others hope that their heritage country will change one day. These small things will make an impact. Because in this election, every vote matters.

In 2020 when the 10% eligible foreign-born voters increased, the notion that the maximum number of immigrants will support Democrats in 2020 is wrong. For example, the states with the largest number of immigrants, California, New York, Texas, and New Jersey, will vote in higher numbers towards the Republican party. Trump may not win electoral college votes for all the states, but this election is also a battle of popular votes. I spoke of the killing of General Soleimani in the earlier paragraph. Do you know how many Iranian Americans are there? Over **One Million.** And many live in California. This means if 60% of them are voters, then there is a strong chance the freedom-loving Iranians American will vote for Trump and the Republican party. The hypothesis is simple: Every new citizen who has seen him fight for keeping the American Dream alive will need to make a long-term decision in mind.

Naturalized Immigrants (US Citizens) and Illegal Immigrants

When naturalized immigrants achieve and clear their legal status to get citizenship in the United States of America, they have done it the right way. They stood in the line, followed the rules, and did it by the law. When they witness undocumented immigrants coming and gaining from the system, they may feel heartburn (figuratively) comparing with their struggle. Plus, undocumented immigrants may pull down the labor rate, thus reducing employment issues. Just google and see the news about employment fraud and relation to social security numbers. There was a case in Kansas also. Now the United States Supreme Court has passed a judgment allowing states to use criminal laws against illegal immigrants and those who do not have work authorization.

Now there will always be many groups that will not vote Republicans. One such group can be those US citizens who are living with undocumented parents or relatives. They feel a need to vote for Democrats. If the Trump administration comes with a plan to regularize these undocumented immigrants, it can be a game-changer. There were talks of doing this as a layered option. Like limited voting rights. But did not hear much later. Time will tell.

Voting by Citizens who are Foreign-born Immigrants:

In 2020, almost 21 million foreign-born immigrants can cast a vote for the presidential election. In the election of 2016, the voting turnover of foreign-born immigrants was 54%. According to a survey, this turnover will increase in the election of 2020. Due to the increase in foreign immigrants' voting, the election of 2020 can be an example of a game-changer.

Migration and Voting

Many factors contribute to moving from one state to another, whether career enhancement or better living conditions. However, such local migration has wide-ranging implications in the geopolitical scenario of the country. Voting patterns face an indeterminate variable as interstate migration increases. The voter population starts to shift in the traditional Red and Blue states.

Reasons for Interstate Migration

Interstate migration refers to the phenomenon of an individual or household moving from one state and settling into a different state within the U.S. Whether that is for personal or fiscal reasons, millions of Americans move states every year, settling into a new city, and voting in a new district. While there is no fixed way of accounting for individual moves, the number of interstate migrations is often estimated by the IRS tax information that records the taxpayer's address change in the past year. Based on this data, the 2010 Census-estimated nearly 12.9 million interstate migrations annually in the 2000-2009 decade. However, in recent years, this number has almost tripled with a surge of the population moving out of traditionally Liberal states. Young, liberal voters and racial minorities often decide to move away from these high tax states to cities like Houston, Dallas, Atlanta, Phoenix, and Orlando (the southern states). These cities are fast-growing metropolitans with a good standard of living but low taxes. As this happens, red counties have turned blues. Bad ideas and failed policies sometimes follow this migration. But as more people get Red Pilled and people move out of the bubble of fixed thought, migration can lead to more voices been spoken up in favor of President Trump. Suppose those newly migrated citizens to the red states do not alter their views, seeing the big picture. In that case, there is a danger of Trump losing counties, and there will close elections in certain states. The vital thing to do is to communicate, discuss, and spread the red pilling.

The Impact of Migration of Voting patterns

According to the American Community Survey, in 2018, around 32.4 million people (10.1 percent of the recorded population) moved within the United States. This number was primarily concentrated in the South as more and more people migrated there from other areas. States such as Florida and Texas had a net gain of about 512,000 people in their population count in one year. This wide dispersion on the individual level brings benefits to the people. Still, it also dramatically affects the country's macro-political perspective by changing the states' geographical voter concentration.

As we move closer to the 2020 Presidential Election and early voting begins, predictions are rampant regarding the support the political parties will receive from allied states and the wide-ranging results from the Swing states. However, methods like using pre-existing poll results and historical voter concentrations lose their reliability with the constant population movement. Statistics show that we might be seeing a shift in the regular voting patterns as many liberal voters are moving to traditionally conservative cities, possibly overthrowing all convention prediction techniques. But then again, we have seen this picture before. If these new members leave failed states and ideas, they will know the importance of conservative and libertarian values. Their minds may change. Blending of thoughts through discussion is needed.

Trump Administration & African Americans

The USA's constitution's fourteenth amendments elaborate that White and Black Americans are equal at the same place. The theory of white people "Equal but separate" was dismissed after this amendment. There are multiple projects done by Trump's administration for African Americans. It can be a game-changer in the presidential election. Some examples of the projects:

- **Opportunity Zone Investment**: This is the most critical project. Many Black American influencers and leaders confess that this project is an ample opportunity for the community. The government is investing billions of dollars in thousands of areas. Opportunity Zones are projected to attract $100 billion in private investments to the communities. The result should be job opportunities, especially for African Americans. When I read about Baltimore's inundated' with opportunity zone questions (it has 42 zones), these are encouraging signs. This is a work in progress.

- **First Step Act**: This legislation of Trump's administration is the most effective and vital. This legislation will make reforms in jail and jail policies. This act also decreases the imprisonment tenure and put some limits on the punishments for different offenses. According to the First Step Act, jail administration started many rehabilitation projects for the prisons, for example, Jobs, different types of work, Classes, educational courses, etc. This will help the prisons learn something from these courses to start their new life after getting discharged from imprisonment. The First Step Act's accomplishments include:

  - Retroactive application of the Fair Sentencing Act, which reduced the 100 to 1 crack cocaine sentencing disparity. It has benefited over 2,000 people with sentence reductions. The average reduction is nearly 6 years. 91% of persons receiving these reductions are African Americans.

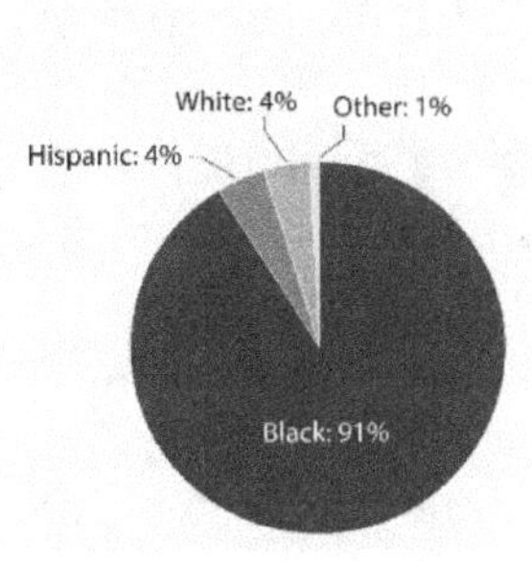

  - 342 people: Approved for the elderly home confinement pilot program.
  - 107 people: Compassionate release with sentence reductions.
  - Expansion of good-time credits implemented in July led to the release of approximately 3,000 in federal prisons; one-third, however, was transferred to the custody of other jurisdictions because of existing detainers.

- **Support to HBCU**: Trump approved financing and projects in support of universities and colleges for HBCU. HBCU stands for Historically black colleges and universities, and there are more than 100 HBCUs. Most of them established before 1964, and they connect with about 300,000 students. Though it is 3% of colleges in the U.S., 20% of black college graduates. The first two-year Trump admin provided a grant of $100 million more in total compared to Obama's first two years. $1.43 billion funding approved in FY 2010, FY 2011 vs. $1.58 billion in FY 2018, 2019. If inflation is considered, it may not be more extensive in value. Nevertheless, those in mainstream media who spoke about Trump's threat and problems for minorities rising should consider this. Trump is a President for all Americans.

- **Before the Pandemic**:
  - o Lowest unemployment rate at Sept 2019 at 5.5%
  - o Poverty rate: lowest since tracking at 18.8%

The pandemic has hit the community hard, and these numbers have changed. But it can be built again. Candidate Trump worked with various African Americans during his business days. And President Trump has shown intent to make a positive impact on African Americans. Changing voting patterns and preference is an indicator. Those are giving in the next chapter.

Trump Administration & Hispanics and Latinos

In November of 2020, with record eligibility of 32 million, the Latinos will be on the top among the minority groups voters. They make up the Electorate's largest ethnic minority. The number exceeds the African American community, which is standing at 30 million eligible voters. Statistically speaking, they make up about 13.3 percent of all eligible voters. What is even more important is that they make up many voters in the swing states. The states of Colorado, Nevada, Arizona, and Florida have many eligible Latino voters. They make up about 1/4th of the total voters in Florida. Therefore it is safe to say that Latino Votes matter a lot in determining the next presidency.

Increasing Trump's support among Latina Voters: This attributed to the practical steps he took for the community's welfare. Mark Leyva, A prominent Latino figure from Indiana, said that his actions are better than any other president's that they'd had in the past despite Donald Trump's rough tweets or comments. He said that the Latino base of The Democratic Party is weakening because Latinos feel that Donald Trump has done everything he said he was going to do. And this has impacted the ordinary citizens. A significant number of Latino Votes being dedicated to the conservative is an established fact. Ever since the "Latinos con Eisenhower" movement started in California in 1950, there have been many Republican Latino Voters. According to these voters, the Hispanics and Latinos' characteristics and their value in family, church, and work are reflected in the Republican policies. Many of the

Republican Latinos see President Trump as a God-Fearing man who values the Christian faith. They feel that they have been ignored by the Democrats for their division of civil rights is mainly in White and Black. President Donald Trump has also won Latino sympathies by pointing out that his administration is making and implementing laws against socialism and communism. The concept is vital and very attractive to a large number of Latino people. The message resonates deeply with the Latino population scarred by the Latin American Autocrats.

To sum things up, though, there is a large community of Hispanics and Latin Americans. They are attracted by campaign messages regarding the economy, like free enterprise and low taxes. There is also the profound significance of social issues for Hispanics, Many of whom are catholic but increasingly evangelical.

Another block is the Asian communities. I will share my views around the Indian communities. There are close to 2 million Indian Americans (Indian heritage) citizens. They had given strong support to Prime Minister Modi of India when he visited the United States during the Texas meet up. President Trump has been supportive (a lot) of India in a different area – Defense, Economy, sharing technologies, etc. Also, his views resonate more closer to the Indian government compared to Harris or Democrats. This group will play a role in close elections.

US Armed Forces Personnel and Law Enforcement Officers:

Armed Forces Personnel: There are close to 1.35 million active service personnel across the six service components. Yes, six, the last one is Space Force, don't forget that – something as a marker for the future. There are also close to 800,000 reserves. This gives a total of 2.15 million. Within this group, they are also immigrants who are working. Together with families (and extended families), this is a big group of a voting bloc. But it does not end here. There is a large veteran group of over two million servicemen and servicewomen who have given their best days for their country. With a total of 4.15 million personnel and taking their families into account (average family size of 3.14, and if we take a number, say 3), then this group of around 12 million connected members. So a 10-15 million bloc.

This is a significant voting bloc. This voting block is a bloc who makes continuous sacrifices want to see the flag been respected. For the families, patriotism is there, and also the wish for endless wars to end. But there is pride always in this

Law Enforcement Personnel: This is another voting block that helps build President Trump's popular Presidential vote. And they and their families will vote in higher numbers to President Trump due to his support for law enforcement officers and the sacrifices they make. They are close to 700,000 of them, and with families and (equivalent) retired officers – this bloc can consist of over 4 million.

Now I am not saying these offices have a political bias or will now follow the law. Those on the center and leaning democrat may move towards voting for President Trump based on his policies towards the nation, law enforcement, and their views on the nature of protests they see around. Remember, a few officers have fallen, their peers. They are like family together. Where they go one, they go all for their family and children.

WWG1WGA: *Movie reference,* part of a prop in White Squall.

WWG1WGA is an acronym for Where We Go One We Go All. These words (WWG1WGA) was inscribed in a bell in a boat in the movie White Squall. The bell shown in the movie serves both as an acoustic signal during foggy weather. It also indicates the length of the chain during an anchoring maneuver. It also can indicate the time of day when someone clings it. When 5pm, there will be seventeen clings?

CHAPTER 9
Battle Grounds | 4D Chess

Strong or lean. Toss-up or battleground. These are terms that we have seen and heard over the many years. There have been changes where a lean towards one party went to another, or a strong, become lean. These changes happened due to change in demographics, changing voting population, and the state's evolving nature (plus in few counties, illegal immigrants as voters, but this is a different discussion). Now see the following table, which has been mapped by CNN (Oct 8th, 2020). The states which are in bold are the one which Trump won in 2016. And you can see that CNN never learns.

Strong Democratic	Lean Democratic	Toss-Up	Lean Republican	Strong Republican
California (55), Connecticut (7) Delaware (3) DC (3) Hawaii (4) Illinois (20) Maine (3) Maryland (10) Massachusetts (11) New Jersey (14) New Mexico (5) New York (29) Oregon (7) Rhode Island (4) Vermont (3) Virginia (13) Washington (12)	**Arizona (11)** Colorado (9) **Michigan (16)** Minnesota (10) Nebraska 2nd Congressional District (1) Nevada (6) New Hampshire (4) **Pennsylvania (20)** **Wisconsin (10)**	**Florida (29)** **Georgia (16)** **Iowa (6)** **Maine 2nd Congressional District (1)** **N Carolina (15)** **Ohio (18)**	Texas (38)	**Alabama (9)** **Alaska (3)** **Arkansas (6)** **Idaho (4)** **Indiana (11)** **Kansas (6)** **Kentucky (8)** **Louisiana (8)** **Mississippi (6)** **Missouri (10)** **Montana (3)** **Nebraska (4)** **N Dakota (3)** **Oklahoma (7)** **S. Carolina (9)** **S. Dakota (3)** **Tennessee (11)** **Utah (6)** **W Virginia (5)** **Wyoming (3)**
203	87	85	38	125

What we see here is mainstream media, and those poll agencies who failed big time last year still have not learned. I use this as a base to discuss my points. There are deeply entrenched voters on both sides of the points of view. The minority voters – African Americans (~13.4%) and Hispanics (~18%) will make a big difference. They are present in many states where they will influence the electoral college votes. Trump got 28% of Hispanic votes and around 6% Black votes. These two groups (31.9%), if they swing 10% towards Trump, many counties will turn red from the blue currently. The popular vote also will change.

Increasing support among Hispanic and Latin American Voters:

For the first time in history, Latinos are the largest minority group of eligible voters. They are occupying the record eligibility of 32 million, which is greater than 30 million African Americans. In 104 U.S. counties, they make up at least 50% of the population. While many Latino voters are Republic owing to the simple fact that they belong to the church. Increasing numbers of catholic and particularly evangelical votes are undoubtedly Trump's. Along with that, many of the Hispanics and Latin Americans support Trump for their number one concern and priority is the Economy. They are attracted to the messages of free enterprise and low taxes.

One particular way Trump's campaign has been gaining attention is his emphasis on anti-socialism and anti-communism policies. His claims hit a chord, especially with Hispanics who have come from countries like Cuba and Venezuela. These people have been scarred by socialist regimes and are completely against it. Trump's campaign has been amazingly effective in this regard. That is why Democrats cannot rely on getting Cuban votes that they had obtained easily before. In addition to that, there is Miami Dade County, Florida's most populous and once Democratic bastion where now Trump has many voters. It is one of the reasons Trump's campaign is so sure that they will get Florida.

In the 2016 US presidential Elections, the Edison Research for the National Election Pool's exit polls showed that President Donald Trump won 28% of the Latino Vote. Today, Four years later, many more Latinos are willing to vote for Preside Trump. Now the national polls show that Trump will get about 30% of the Latino population votes. According to the New Polls, in one of Florida's top battleground states, Trump is leading. A new NBC News/Marist poll shows President Donald Trump is gaining ground on Vice President Joe Biden; Trump has a lead among Latino voters, 50% to 46%.

Democrats have a reason to be anxious because even in Florida's most populous Miami-Dade County, the one which has been a Democratic bastion, Trump has a significant number of voters among the Latinos. It is essentially neck and neck at 47 percent to 46 percent, according to a Bendixen and Amandi Poll. Many Democrats are concerned that the Cuban Votes they had easily won in the past are now very much out of their hands. In a critical battleground state like Florida, these votes have the power to change the end scene completely.

Increased Support by African Americans

In 2016, though Trump got 6% of black votes, most of these votes were men at 16%. Black women's votes were less than 2%. This is where a strong impact has been made. As more black conservative voices speak up, as more discussion around the pros and cons are discussed, as more free-minded communication happens without fear of judgment, the counties will swing first. And then the states will turn towards President Trump and Republicans. Recent surveys have indicated this.

In a Hill-HarrisX poll conducted in the Republican National Convention, it was seen Support for President Donald Trump has also increased among the African American community. Compared with a survey of registered black voters conducted on August 8-11, where the President received 15 percent support from the group, the survey conducted on Aug 22-25 depicted 24 percent support. That is a significant rise of 9 points. But a more crucial 18-point rise since 2016. Even if there is a 50% accuracy issue – the support to Donald Trump will be in double digits. As a base case, the support is doubled from 6% last time to 12%. So, this is X million, new voters. The increasing support in minority groups might very well lead to Donald Trump winning the 2020 presidential elections.

Reverse Bradley Effect

Bradley Effect is the observed discrepancies between voter opinion polls and election outcomes. It was theorized and named after the California Governor elections in 1982. In this election, Tom Bradley (Black Candidate), the long-term mayor of Los Angeles, had the polls in his favor. But he did not win the election. The election was won by Republican candidate George Deukmejian. The reason was that most voters did not share their minds in front of media and poll companies as they don't want to be inferred with discrimination. This impact was again seen 1992 Senate Election in Illinois, and they are more examples. It is said Barrack Obama, during his Presidential Campaign, faced both Bradley Effect and the Reverse Bradley effect. Which means people who wanted to vote for him said they will not vote for him. But voting for him ultimately in the ballot box.

This reverse Bradley effect will happen a lot in the Trump case. They were many voters who did not want to say they would vote for him but did. The voters of Trump did not like to share it out in the open due to mainstream media bias. But there will be many African Americans and Hispanics who may say they do not want to vote for him but will do. This is something that happened earlier and will still happen.

OS for OM, Possible California Shock:

Can California go OS for OM, Orange State for Orange Man? Many of the Trump supporters are claiming that Trump will win California. Recent polls have shown Trump's rising popularity in California, though it's not all the way through. Some call it A California Surprise or a California Shock that will surely carve another pathway to victory for Donald Trump. But will it possible. There is nothing impossible, but I see California as a path to gain a more popular vote. As you read in the keys that Democrat has a 5-6 million advantage over Republicans in two states – New York and California. Last time Trump's popular vote in California was around 3.4 million. Taking this out, Trump won the popular vote. Such was a foresight of the Founding Fathers, and the importance of Electoral College Votes is known now. No one state or a few cities should decide the future of the entire nation.

Coming back to California, what I wanted to understand to is there a way Trump can win more votes than last time? Can he make inroads into minority hearts and minds, and they vote for him? In this chapter, I have already shared how African American and Hispanic voters give a more positive job approval to President Trump than candidate Trump four years earlier. A vital point to note is that the Hispanics are not minorities (population-wise). In fact, in 18 counties, they are above 40% of the population. And Candidate Trump had won 6 of these counties!!! That is a 33% strike rate. This shows that there are a group of Hispanics and Latinos who have voted for Trump in 2016, and more will do in 2020. Such changes can provide President Trump more boost to the popular vote.

To understand this better, I have developed seven archetypes for California (taking 2016 data). These archetypes are group based on specific qualitative and quantitative grouping. The objective to understand what Trump can get more votes. Yup for Orange man, the orange state, I used types of different oranges. Now coming to details of the data. Here are they:

	Archetype Name	Description
A	Clementine	**Engaged Counties for Trump** *Counties where Republican supports, increased in points*
B	Navel	**Diverse Engaged Counties for Trump** *Counties with a large Hispanic population (> that CA avg)*
C	Blood	**Disappointed with Trump** *Counties which Swung positive R to D* **or Reduced R**
D	Bergamot	**Democrat Counties diverse Not So Strong Hold** *Counties with close elections population voting D*
E	Valencia	**Democrat Counties not diverse Strong Hold** *Counties with white population voting D*
F	Seville	**Democrat diverse Strong Hold** *Counties with a highly diverse population*
G	Tangelo	**Democrat diverse II Strong Hold** *Counties with large minorities (but less Hispanic, Black)*

There are two groups of counties where Republicans are entrenched. The archetypes are Clementine (A) and Navel (B). Apart from this, many counties had voted big for Republicans in 2012 and 2008 but did not go for Trump in 2016. Reasons can be many, but I am willing to bet they will turn around and vote for him now. These counties are grouped Blood orange archetype (C). In terms of population, A+B+C covers 25% of the state. What will get interesting is when counties in Bergamot (D) & Valencia (E) will start voting in a larger number for Trump. When that happens, we are closer to 40% of the state population. With law and order (and not Russia Russia) and Economy on the ballot, President Trump will make good inroads in San Francisco and Los Angeles. That is my hypothesis. And don't forget the Middle East and Asians – Iranians, Israelis, and Indians. They will add a more popular vote. There are more details in the tables on the next page.

Trump's campaign and he are optimistic that they can make inroads into California. If that indeed turns out to be accurate, Biden will be in a huge pickle. California is not a monolithic blue state, as some belief. The results on election day can surprise if the Californian Republicans come out and vote for Trump. This is where the Charisma Key comes into play. Someone put a Hollywood styled TRUMP sign also. Though it was taken out, Trump supporters are coming out and voicing in larger numbers. This is the power of Charisma. Ability to motivate voters to get the message across.

Orange State for Orange Man

The following details are taken from 2016

		# of Counties	Population	% Hispanic	% Black	% White	Other Demo %
A	Clementine	15	7,87,032	13%	2%	77%	8.2%
B	Navel	7	9,72,519	53%	3%	37%	7.3%
C	Blood	7	78,01,393	40%	4%	42%	14.1%
D	Bergamot	5	32,01,382	47%	7%	38%	8.7%
E	Valencia	7	12,53,678	22%	2%	67%	9.4%
F	Seville	10	1,61,27,997	44%	7%	34%	15.1%
G	Tangelo	7	79,22,919	23%	8%	40%	29.2%

		# of Counties	Median Income	% College Educated	Unemployment	Avg. Trump Vote %	Avg. Hillary Vote %
A	Clementine	15	45,292	18.4%	7.8%	59.3%	33.9%
B	Navel	7	46,186	12.9%	11.0%	56.1%	38.1%
C	Blood	7	60,795	25.0%	6.8%	48.4%	45.6%
D	Bergamot	5	48,438	17.0%	7.9%	43.8%	49.9%
E	Valencia	7	61,550	30.7%	5.9%	28.2%	64.4%
F	Seville	10	60,852	24.0%	8.3%	32.1%	62.3%
G	Tangelo	7	23%	8%	4.7%	22.3%	72.0%

Opinion Battleground:

Since the very beginning, politicians have used negative propaganda against their opponents. In the modern world, the term used for this phenomenon is the "Smear Campaign." Smear campaigning is a premeditated, well thought out and strategic use of lies, false accusations, dramatization, and suspicions against an individual to destroy their credibility. It is a deliberate effort to destroy the reputation of a person. President Trump has faced many smear campaigns against him from Russia Hoax to fake stories that can fill an encyclopedia. As the declass happened now, the real truth will come out.

In 2017, in answer to a reporter's question regarding the use of smear campaigning against Trump in the context of his relations with Russia, Nancy Pelosi described 'smear politics' as a diversionary tactic. It is also called a **wrap-up smear**. She said that it is a well-known tactic where you smear someone with falsehoods and then merchandise it. As soon as it starts circulating in media and is reported in the press, 'they' have the validation that the press reported it. She further commented that the term is self-evident and blatantly self-serving. She also said that it is beyond the normal competition, and the press enjoys it. All because they never thought she would lose.

So what President Trump is up against is a battleground of opinions against him. And he has given us what he is against. There is a period where Donald Trump visited stadiums. In all (of what I saw) places, he was cheered, and chants of USA-USA-USA boomed from the audience. But one place, I remember booing happened. Which place? It was in Washington DC, aka the suited swamp. This, I felt, was a way Trump was sending coms to Annons what he is facing. This is what his supporters and all the citizens are facing. This Deep State is ably supported by propaganda news channels or, as Donald Trump likes to call them, Fake News – The Enemies of the People.

4D Chess: A word *from Urban Dictionary*

The world is a game on stage, and we are the actors. And in this stage, a lot of complex mind games go on. 4D-Chess is a multi-layered strategy that no one outside of the gamer's mind has an idea of the moves and counter moves. And the outcome becomes clear after weeks, months, or years.

CHAPTER 10
4th vs. 5th Estate | Fake News Mockingbird

There is no operative press in the United States, just a bunch of interlocking interests to push forward an agenda. They are weapons of mass deception

Suppose you are still one of the people who believe that the news media is a reliable source of narrative for your daily headlines for what is going on in the world. In that case, chances are that you are one of the few people remaining who do so. From the inception of modern journalism in the early twentieth century, the road has been nothing but revolutionary. With more and more power to the media, modern journalism can have on the tide's (opinion) direction cannot be underestimated. In recent years, however, this impact might not have been unbiased.

The Fourth Estate

The fourth estate, aptly named after the media, found its place as the fourth founding member of society after judicial, legislative, and executive bodies, applied to the mass media that we see as journalism. The media's role was apparent: give the facts to the people as seen, without political, social, or religious biases, free of judgment and meant to educate. What A JOKE! Nothing can be far from the truth now. News is like the arm of a propaganda machine. It is like the Nazi or Stalin or Mao news channel going on. In the US constitution, the Fifth amendment grants the Fourth estate freedom of practice from the government or any higher authorities. What happened then? As the question arises: if the media is free to speak, is it free of judgment?

The Changing Role of the Media

In recent years, the public's trust in modern media is on a steady decline. According to the Gallop organization, only 41% of the American public has believed in the contemporary media narrative, compared to 72% of people in 1976. This decline in the last few decades is due to several incidents, including negative coverage of particular political and social events, opinionated views of events, and a heavily controlled narrative against people's needs.

President Trump has been entangled in media controversies since the start of his presidency and is very vocal about the steps modern journalism needs to take to appear professional. Because the bias is extensive and continuously give him negative coverage. It looks the fourth estate is for gaslighting the public.

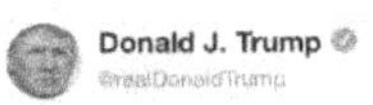

This opinionated form of mass media is not new under scrutiny. Even during the reign of the former president, the reliability of the media was questionable. According to the Atlantic, when asked about Fox News in 2010, these were views of the former president: 'Obama made clear that he believes the channel's "opinionated" reporting is "ultimately destructive for the long-term growth" of the country.' (Well, something big is coming out now called Truth).

Perhaps the problem lies with the fact that the fourth estate does not stop at just stating an opinion on a topic. Instead, it enhances that opinion, disregards the opposing views, and often convolutes the facts to present an image that supports their opinion. The emergence of some 'fake news' agencies has added to the fire of mistrust the public already holds for the media. This fake news, aimed at defamation and miscommunication, presents in the mainstream media and through social media, which has a broader target audience, highlighting personal propaganda and reducing the journalism industry's reliability.

Rise of the Fifth Estate

There has always been a need for honest media that connect the public to the world's more comprehensive affairs. Considering the disconnect in the way the Fourth estate represents mainstream journalism, the rise of the Fifth estate might be better to tackle these issues. This media, consisting of personal and organizational views that present an outlier perspective of events (the non-mainstream media per se). Through the primary medium of blogging and social media journalism, the Fifth estate brings more open views that are often free of political agendas, hence are more preferred by the people. These are rich in opinions and discourse.

The improvement in technology and global connectivity has made it easier for people to research and voice personal opinions rather than rely on mainstream journalism for the facts. Rather than focusing on any one media outlet, the Fifth estate brings out a varied mindset that brings forward the community's thoughts and the general public into the light. Through channels like Facebook, Twitter, or YouTube, people can now influence public opinion and present their views for consideration.

A Change of Narrative

Along with bringing a change in the mass media narrative, the Fifth estate highlights the democratic nature to a more individual level. These journalists' influence outside of the traditional media networks is just as crucial in shaping the country's political and social tide. The mainstream media may present opinionated dialogue under the pretense of facts. The new narrative holds no pretensions and states the opinions as is. The people know what they are in for, and they have the power to choose what to listen to.

The Future of the Media

In the world of consumerism, the content we consume is highly specific too. Whether that is the mainstream journalism or the new Fifth estate media, the content that the public is presented with plays a substantial role in forming our opinions and world view. As such, responsible content consumption should be the duty of the people. So, despite the varying opinions presented in the mainstream or non-traditional media, the ability to perceive, filter, and evaluate information is the key to a better communication system.

Fake News Mockingbird: *A term for today and a CIA plan*

Mockingbird was a CIA operation whose objective was to manipulate news media for propaganda purposes. The means were infiltration, training and now look like direct recruitment. In 1975 the Church Committee Congressional investigation showed a direct link between the CIA with media and civic groups. This is a sort of creation of the fifth column and providing Deep State support.

CHAPTER 11
Fifth Column | Thought Crime

The fifth column is a secretive faction or community of provocative and disruptive individuals trying to undermine a nation's solidarity from within by any and all means at their disposal. Their activities are usually in favor of an outside enemy group. Their actions are often clandestine but can be overt as well. The term's origin is traced back to the Spanish civil war (1936-39). The nationalist general Emilio Mola Vidal moved on Madrid with his four army columns and boasted of having a fifth column of his militant supporters within the capital, working to undermine the loyalist government from within.

The term was coined not so long ago. However, there are stories of the existence of such forces scattered throughout history. Every culture, religion, nation, and country has suffered at the hands of such forces at some time in their history. The results of the activities of the fifth column group activities are devastating for the host country.

The fundamental tactics of the fifth column:

The fifth column's tactic repeated throughout history is the secret supporters' infiltration into the nation's very fabric. Various key post to the defense and nation's policymaking is under their influence and control (sounds familiar). The results are apparent. The country's defenses are superficial, and unrest from within caused by the spread of rumors and false information makes it susceptible to even minor attacks. Therefore, whether it is military, political, or commercial, no aspect is safe from the enemy. History walk now:

- In the late 1930s, It became imminent that America would be embroiled in Europe's war. The term fifth column was used to refer to the potential sedition and treason within the United States. The turmoil increased with France's fall in the 1940s as it was blamed on the fifth column, the secret sympathizers of Germany.

- The term fifth column gained more popularity in the 1940s and '50s as it was associated with the Nazi sympathizers and communists. In the Life magazine issue of June 1940, several photos were published with the ominous title "Signs of Nazi Fifth Column" are Everywhere."

- In the same month, the then prime minister of the UK, Winston Churchill, stated that with the parliament's power, fifth column activists' activities will be stopped.

- As Norway was invaded by the Nazis, Vidkun Quisling, a pro-Nazi military officer, and politician declared a new fascist government in Norway with himself as the PM. His name Quisling became synonymous with traitor or collaborator

- The Philippine campaign, also known as the fall of the Philippine, taking place from Dec 8th, 1941 to May 8th,, 1942 was the invasion of the Philippines by Imperial Japan. During this invasion, the large population of Japanese immigrants, acting as the fifth column, welcomed the invasion. The first attack on Davao was assisted by the fifth columnist's residents of the area.

- In many Western countries, the Counter-Jihad Movement portrays immigrant Muslims as the fifth column and an existential threat to the West.

- In the late 1990s, the existence of a secret army created by the Central Intelligence Agency, with the code name Operation Gladio came to light. It was created during the 1950s to combat a Soviet invasion of western Europe. The disclosure of a clandestine paramilitary group networking throughout Europe is an excellent example of Fifth Column Activities. Since its exposure, many European officials have described similar operations in many of the NATO countries.

- In 2014, The Ukrainian revolution took place in Ukraine. After a series of violent protests, police riots, and unknown shootings in Kyiv's capital, the elected government was overthrown. The elected president ousted. There was suspicion of a robust fifth column of Deep State (Cabal)

History of Fifth Column in the United States:

The United States has a history of the fifth column as well. While many people attribute many suspicions of fifth column activities to mere conspiracy theories, many people believe that the fifth column activists have controlled the United States' national and international affairs since the beginning. Some examples from history are around Nazi sympathizers. But the truth is darker, and I will not talk about it in the current book. Let us understand now.

Recent Times and Deep States Conspiracy:

The term Deep state has been used on multiple occasions by President Donald Trump. In fact, a major part of his Election campaign is devoted to his fight against these deep states. He has referred to them as unelected operatives who defy the voters' choice to push their own secret agendas. The term has created its own following like some secretive Illuminati organization. It is the real power behind the curtains. In Donald Trump's narrative, this is composed of bureaucracy and civil servants. As the presidents come and go every four years, these are the people who will stay for decades and play their part in shaping the country's policy-making, the national and the international affairs. Trump claims that these individuals are "holdovers" from the prior administrations, working on their own personal schemes and blocking his agenda and policies. Trump has repeatedly declared this in his rallies all over the country.

While the bureaucracy holds undeniable power in the United States of America, the question being asked is how valid Trump's claims that the deep states are running their own agenda instead of being loyal to America only are. However, the important thing is that Donald Trump is not the only President to be suspicious and deeply skeptical of the 'deep states.' As the elections are nearing, Donald Trump's claims regarding his fight against deep states are picking up pace as well. Meanwhile, the critics point out that Donald Trump is trying to delegitimize any voices of disagreements by embroiling the U.S. government's civil servants in some conspiracy theory. The question to ask is why we cannot solve many problems after so many years of no world wars and a somewhat functioning democracy.

Thought Crime: *Book reference, 1984*

This word is from the dystopian novel, Nineteen Eighty-Four. The government in the novel is Ingsoc (English Socialism). If someone is having politically different thoughts, even if it is unspoken, it is a crime. No free thoughts are allowed. With such an environment, free thinkers will not survive. Future, there can be vPC, Violent Political Correctness with a dictionary of what can be spoken and thought.

CHAPTER 12
Stopping Trump | Deep State

Can America's democracy be threatened? Can a group of members work together to make this happen? The question to ask first, has democracy been threatened before? Yes, it has. A history of countries has lost its democracy to enter a period that had a military dictatorship, socialism, or communist governments. There was also a revolution where people came on the streets, challenged the governments, and toppled them. Few examples of the latter are the Arab Spring in Egypt, the Jasmine Revolution in Tunisia, the fall of the eastern Europe communist bloc. Some of these revolutions have been called as a color revolution. What has been seen in the last few years has been a new sub-segment in such a revolution. A revolution in which foreign players (such as NGOs) investing time, funding, and creating opinions. One example is Ukraine. There was an Orange revolution in 2004-5. And then there was the 2014 Ukrainian revolution, which saw the elected President leave the country. The capital city was besieged by protestors (where his core supporters did not reside). Yes, there was foreign interference (covert and over)—a lot to say here. But just giving highlights. In short, Democracy can be challenged.

Now coming back to the United States. Can this happen here? Will it be in the open? To be honest, I was surprised to find the answer as a YES (sort of). It may be a different variant, but a gaming scenario was carried out in a project in the public eye. This project name is the **Transition Integrity Project. A**s I like to call it, the Deep State backup plan if Democrats do not win the 2020 elections.

Free and Fair Elections

There are huge concerns (via mainstream media) regarding the 2020 presidential elections' legitimacy and the peaceful transition of power. My view is that there still has not been a peaceful transition of power of the 2016 election, which Donald Trump won. This point, I will bring it later in the chapter but let us see 2020 now. As the US presidential elections are being held during the widespread pandemic, there are concerns that voting in person is not possible or safe.

There is already a movement to ensure voting is done virtue of vote by mail. The process has its challenges. Mismanagement and suspected activities at certain touchpoints can cause issues of rigging. The fact that the elections' results might not be clear for days or even weeks after the election day are reasons to cause suspicion and distrust. There have already been cases of this recorded, and FBI and various law enforcement departments are investigating such cases. With certain states having a battleground status or toss-up and close elections in these places, there is a chance of either party contesting the results. Both campaigns will explore legal ambiguities in these states, such as Wisconsin, Pennsylvania, Michigan, and North Carolina. These are the states where the governors are Democrats, but the legislature is under the authority of Republicans. If Florida (2020) chads were an issue, this time, it would be a legal battle in the courts and potentially protests (violent in some cases) on the streets. In these circumstances, it is unlikely for either of the campaigns to concede. A peaceful transition (or continuation of the incumbent) can be a challenge.

Concerns Raised by the Trump supporters:

- They were concerns regarding the Obama administration's attack on Trump via 'Crossfire Hurricane,' a counterintelligence investigation to explore Trump's possible ties with Russia. (This was all hogwash, and more details are being released on how Trump was targeted.)

- Another attempt to harm his 2020 elections are considered to be the Muller Investigations. Robert Muller carried out a special counsel investigation into the suspected Russian interference with the 2016 United States elections. Result of it: no collusion.

- Impeachment of Donald Trump: This was initiated on Dec 18, 2019, on the charges of abuse of power and obstruction of Congress. However, he was acquitted of these charges.

- Even if Trump wins by a landslide majority, the Democrats are unwilling to accept the defeat and concede to the results. The Democrats are preparing for riots on election day and even anarchy if the results are not liking. There have been various claims in which left-wing supporters, termed as the 'leading progressive groups,' have been preparing for mass protests and violence if Biden loses the presidential elections or does not concede.

Concerns raised by the Biden Supporters:

- Trump has on multiple occasions and quite publicly refused to accept the election results. He has been giving conflicting statements regarding the validity of the mail ballots. Though he has voted by mail in the past, he claims that mail ballots are prone to fraud and duplicity.

- The Democrats claim that Trump's conflicting statements are part of his election scheme to provide grounds for his election fraud allegations later on. They believe that Biden has a decisive advantage. Biden has been encouraging people to use mail ballots to stay safe in the pandemic.

- There have also been attempts to delay the elections on account of unspecified and unsubstantiated voter fraud.

The Transition Integrity Project

Considering the circumstances, in June 2020, an initiative was taken. The objective was to prevent the disruption of presidential elections and ensure a peaceful transition of power. The project, named The Transition Integrity Project, congregated a bipartisan (really?) group of more than a hundred participants. They were current and former senior government officials and campaign leaders, academics, journalists, polling, and other experts, nearly making up the United States of America's think tank. And they all took part in a series of crisis planning exercises that some call "the war games."

Initial Convention of Transition Integrity Project:

The transition integrity project was initiated in late 2019, first assembled by Rosa Brooks and Nils Gilman. Rosa Brooks is serving as the Scott K. Ginsburg Professor of Law and Policy. She is also a former pentagon senior official, a journalist, an author, and a foreign policy expert. Nils Gilman is the former Vice-Chancellor of the University of California and a historian at Berggruen Institute. Some of the prominent names of the transition integrity project beside the founders are Michael Steele, a former chair of the national committee; John Podesta, former White House Chief of Staff to former President of United States Bill Clinton; Jennifer Granholm, former Michigan Governor; former Kentucky secretary of state Trey Grayson, Journalists William Kristol, Edward Luce, Max Boot, and David Frum, and others.

The War Games:

The members of the Transition Integrity Project held simulations, the so-called war games, in their virtual meetings for four days over two weeks in the late summer. These war games were designed to explore every possible way the presidential elections might end in the post-election crisis. In these war game scenarios, Biden was played by John Podesta. The latter was a former top aide to President Barack Obama and Former Chief of Staff to President Bill Clinton. President Trump's role was played by David Frum, a Canadian American political commentator from the Republican party. Bill Kristol, a neoconservative political analyst and political commentator on various networks, was also a Republican. The four scenarios were played out and examined by the TIP. These scenarios were

Scenario/Game One: Ambiguous Results

The first scenario that was played and investigated was the one where neither party had a clear win. The final outcome depended on the results of three states, Michigan, Florida, and North Carolina. The combinations could end up in different ways, including a 269-269 Electoral College tie or a blue shift. The ballots are destroyed in one of the states, and the results from others are disputed. In any case, the results are ambiguous, and the winner of the presidential elections remains unclear.

Conclusion or the outcome: Neither party is willing to yield, there is no resolution of conflict, and both parties are claiming victory even in the joint session of Congress held on January 6. There are high hostility and two claims to Commander-in-Chief's power, including access to the nuclear codes. (Preventing a Disrupted Presidential Election, 2020)

Scenario/Game Two: A Clear Biden Win:

Biden achieves a clear victory by winning both the Electoral College and the Popular Vote. The outcome of this scenario was initial allegations of fraud by the Trump campaign. When the allegations didn't stick, Trump took steps to benefit himself and his family, politically, legally, and financially.

Conclusion or the outcome: The white house is ultimately handed over to Biden. Finally, the Trump Campaign moved ahead to appoint either Donald Trump himself or his son Donald Trump Jr. to run for presidential elections in 2024.

Scenario/Game Three: A Clear Trump Win:

The third scenario played out so that Trump won the electoral college comfortably, 286 to 252. Still, the conflict arose with the popular vote win. The former vice president and current presidential candidate Joe Biden earned himself a significant popular vote win 52% to 47%. In this scenario, Joe Biden did not concede. Biden threatened and insisted that the house of representatives reject the election results and declare him the Victor. In any case, the gameplay ended in a total constitutional crisis and threats of secession. There were political havoc and danger of rampage, violence, and assaults on the streets along with actual instances of sporadic barbaric incidents. The media was running rampant with antagonistic, aggressive, highly partisan, and unconstrained information. *Conclusion or the outcome:* One outcome of this crisis was an utter decline into authoritarianism. The other significant outcome of the crisis was a change in the democratic set of rules, which entirely eradicated the electoral college to ensure the **popular will prevail.**

Scenario/Game 4: A Narrow Biden Win:

The fourth and final scenario plays out. Biden takes the lead with less than 1% of the popular votes and is predicted to win with a slim lead of 278 electoral votes. The media's role is noteworthy. Fox News is one of the major networks that called the election for Biden. Trump's campaign does not concede and sows conflict and disruption and fierce contest issues. Eventually, the Senate Republicans and Joint Chiefs of Staff accept Biden's win. It all concludes with an edgy, tense, and contentious but ultimately successful transition of power. Earlier in this scenario, Biden's campaign sought to provide a way for Trump to concede to the presidential election results; however, the democratic party had begun investigations into Trump's criminal activities by the end of it his family.

OUTCOME OF THE GAMES:

After conducting various scenarios, the transition integrity project declared that the conclusions were alarming. They claimed that there is a high possibility that the election results will be followed by legal battles, a contested outcome where both the parties refuse to concede, violence on the streets, and even the so-called constitutional impasse.

CRITICISM

The Transition Integrity Project has faced many criticisms by the Trump loyalists (rational and logical). Many are naming the transition integrity project- The ridiculous wargaming of the 2020 elections. Though the Transition integrity project is supposedly composed of both parties, it only included disaffected Republicans. Of the 67 players, many were high-profile critics of Donald Trump, including law professors, retired military officers, former senior US officials, political strategists, and attorneys. The project was funded by the former members of the Obama administration.

There is heavy criticism that the only scenario where the defeated side does not concede a clear win by the other side was Trump's scenario clearly winning the electoral college. In a clear Trump win scenario, the Biden campaign threatens to compromise the constitution, ensuring a constitutional crisis and secession threats by various western states.

The threat of anarchy:

Whatever the 2020 US presidential election outcome is, a peaceful transition does not seem to be on the horizon. With both the campaigns threatening and blaming the other party for planning future violence, the outlook does not appear peaceful.

In the conclusions drawn by the transition integrity project, it's almost a foregone conclusion that riots and violent clashes on the streets will occur if Biden does not win by a landslide majority. In the multiple game scenarios played, the very real threats of Election violence, constitutional crisis, and the secession of western states from the Union were portrayed. No matter how the end of the election, these threats are real, and if the cards are not played right, and

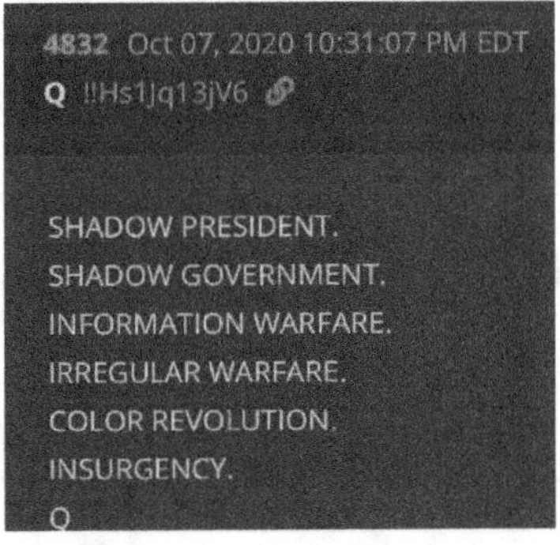

the mass violence gets out of hand, it might result in Anarchy and Civil war where the damage would be out of hand and unpredictable, unlike the war games.

So do go to the next page and see how the initial days of Russian collusion hoax was looking.

DIRECTOR OF NATIONAL INTELLIGENCE
WASHINGTON, DC

SEP 2 9 2020

The Honorable Lindsey Graham
Chairman, Committee on the Judiciary
United States Senate
290 Russell Senate Office Building
Washington, D.C. 20510

Chairman Graham,

In response to your request for Intelligence Community (IC) information related to the Federal Bureau of Investigation's (FBI) Crossfire Hurricane Investigation, I have declassified the following:

- In late July 2016, U.S. intelligence agencies obtained insight into Russian intelligence analysis alleging that U.S. Presidential candidate Hillary Clinton had approved a campaign plan to stir up a scandal against U.S. Presidential candidate Donald Trump by tying him to Putin and the Russians' hacking of the Democratic National Committee. The IC does not know the accuracy of this allegation or the extent to which the Russian intelligence analysis may reflect exaggeration or fabrication.

- According to his handwritten notes, former Central Intelligence Agency Director Brennan subsequently briefed President Obama and other senior national security officials on the intelligence, including the "alleged approval by Hillary Clinton on July 26, 2016 of a proposal from one of her foreign policy advisors to vilify Donald Trump by stirring up a scandal claiming interference by Russian security services."

- On 07 September 2016, U.S. intelligence officials forwarded an investigative referral to FBI Director James Comey and Deputy Assistant Director of Counterintelligence Peter Strzok regarding "U.S. Presidential candidate Hillary Clinton's approval of a plan concerning U.S. Presidential candidate Donald Trump and Russian hackers hampering U.S. elections as a means of distracting the public from her use of a private mail server."

As referenced in his 24 September 2020 letter to your Committee, Attorney General Barr has advised that the disclosure of this information will not interfere with ongoing Department of Justice investigations. Additional declassification and public disclosure of related intelligence remains under consideration; however, the IC welcomes the opportunity to provide a classified briefing with further detail at your convenience.

Respectfully,

Deep State: *Books, Movie and Governance reference*

The words "Deep State" refer to a state within a state, which means a group of entrenched members of the bureaucracy, law, political working together to form a tight network of power that thrives on loyalty. They operate independently with their own agenda and goals and influence political and social decisions.

CHAPTER 13
Factor 17 – Stopping the Deep State | Q

Q is the 17th letter of the English language alphabet. But for many, it is a sign of hope. For some, it is a threat. And for the rest, it is "Are you serious?" or "so what?". So, what is Q or Q anon? According to mainstream media, Q has positioned a mega conspiracy theory, which builds upon many other conspiracy theories. What is been said by various mainstream channels and media is that Qanon can be summarized by what is written in Wikipedia.

According to Wikipedia
QAnon is a far-right conspiracy theory alleging that a cabal of Satan-worshiping pedophiles running a global child sex-trafficking ring is plotting against President Donald Trump, who is battling against the cabal, leading to a "day of reckoning" involving the mass arrest of politicians. Here we have many words. The summary FEATURES given around Q as per wiki are here (we will revisit later in the chapter):

- **Far-Right**: Far-right politics, also referred to as the extreme right or right-wing extremism. They believe in extremist nationalism, nativist ideologies, and authoritarian tendencies

- **Conspiracy Theory**: A conspiracy theory explains an event or situation that invokes a conspiracy by sinister and influential groups, often political in motivation when other explanations are more probable. The term has a negative connotation, implying that the appeal to a conspiracy is based on prejudice or insufficient evidence.

- **Cabal**: A cabal is a group of people united in some close design, usually to promote their private views or interests in an ideology, state, or other community, often by intrigue and usually unbeknownst to those outside their group.

- **Satan**: Satan, also known as the Devil, is an entity in the Abrahamic religions that seduces humans into sin or falsehood.

- **Pedophile**: A person who is sexually attracted to children.

- **Child Trafficking**: Trafficking of children is a form of human trafficking and is defined by the United Nations as the "recruitment, transportation, transfer, harboring, and/or receipt" kidnapping of a child for the purpose of slavery, forced labor, and exploitation.

Is this all true? Is QAnon a bad influence? On September 25th, 2020, the US Congress had to pass House Resolution 1154, "Condemning QAnon and rejecting the conspiracy theories it promotes." It has been not even three years for Q drops or posts, but it has made such an impact that the US Congress had to pass a resolution condemning it. But condemning it for what? Let me walk you through my journey.

QAnon has been in the public space since 28 October 2017 in the message board called 4Chan. The name of the (anonymous) account in 4Chan is that posting is "Q Clearance Patriot." The name became "Q," among the public. Q clearance is the highest security clearance level, permitting access to secret information (in the Nuclear Regulatory Commission). Here Q keeps dropping posts like breadcrumbs. And cannons follow the story and start combining the posts (baking) to understand the story. The posts are, in most cases, questions for people to search the information out. In fact, many posts have weblinks, tweets, links, and always public sources. So, the things where information is sourced from are open (which begs the question, how dangerous then?)

Coming back to the posts. The first post said Hillary Clinton is going to get arrested. OK. This is something that did not happen in October 2017. And if this were the first thing I saw, I would have said, bullshit. This is a madman rant and a group that does not like Hillary Clinton. But this was not the first post I saw. The first details I got of Q and Qanon was in sometime in May 2018 were talks about human trafficking (children). It spoke of an international ring where children have been trafficked for nefarious and ungodly acts. I was like, ok, this is really bad. Trafficking does happen. But children have been trafficked across borders, and such that it enters the United States. How is that possible? For me, I was like no way. How is this possible? I ignored it. I did not go to the posts or visit 4Chan. These we discussions on twitter.

More tweets were coming into my twitter feed around this topic after a few weeks, and the word adrenochrome. As a pharmacist, I did understand how drugs can impact the human body, and adrenochrome was something I did not know much about. I again kept it at the side. Just read the tweets and did not dig, father. Few more days passed by.

Then some news broke. It was around Allison Mack. She was part of the Smallville TV series. Being a Superman fan and watching a few seasons of Smallville, her name resonated. This was July, and I read she had been arrested sometime in April or so for sex trafficking and racketeering. It was multiple charges. I was like, how come I did not get this new early. Well, I did not dig a lot. I then read about NXIVM, who she was sort of part of, and how this organization ran like a cult. First, what is NXIVM (called as Nexium)? It was a multi-level marketing company and offered seminars through its "Executive Success Programs." personal and professional

Back to the digging now. I started reading and tracking the various stories. According to the news coming out (one expose came out in the New York Times in Oct 2017), it talked about how women got branded and had been like sex slaves. WHAT! I then saw an image of the news which Q had dropped in a tweet. I dug more. One of the accusations (which has been proven true now as the guilty verdict has come) was that there were two groups of inner clubs called DOS and The Vow, which were a part of an inner "sisterhood" of NXIVM. As part

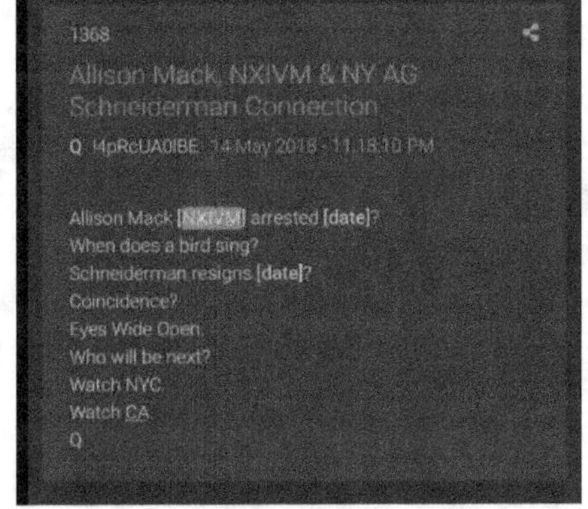

of an initiation, process women were branded and then forced into sexual slavery. Slavery? Are we in medieval times? The stories were in the news for many years. ABC News on Dec 16, 2017, which spoke about this in detail. Now we have a Netflix documentary. So, this is one thing that Q spoke about to wake up people to search for news and stories that impacted the world. Is this anti- anti-Semite or a conspiracy theory? Well, keep reading on.

As more and more NXIVM details came, women spoke of indoctrination with cult-like practices. They spoke of submission and obedience practices. The victims told them they were slaves and had mastered. Those who did not comply and broke the rules were punished. The punishment fasting or worse physical harm. Is this for real? I then thought if this can happen can child trafficking and slavery happen in the open. It was time to go into the rabbit hole.

This is where my real journey began. When I got to know about Q, I was like, "So What?". I thought Q like a group of Americans, hardcore Trump supporters. But after reading the news of NXIVM been confirmed, I started to research on my own. A piece of shocking news came up. It was reported in the print media, but not a lot of coverage given. The news was about **300 Children from India Sold to US Based Clients.** From India to the United States, this child trafficking operation ran for ten years, from 2007 to 2018. The trafficking operating was being conducted in the open with a real passport but the impersonation of those in the passport's identities. In March 2018, the racket was unearthed. The children trafficked were girls from poor families. After the girls reached the United States, the passport would come back to India. It can be a case for sending child labor to the US, maybe for certain restaurants. How did such an operation happen for so long? Why such a crime been committed. This is where I wanted to learn more about the posts.

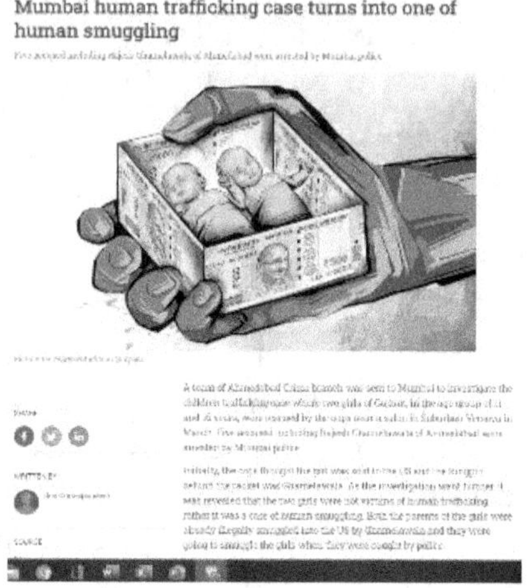

As more days past, more news kept on getting true. There was a term been used in the drops: "Future Proves Past." There were certain things discussed in the drops by Q before it became clear. It was like he was posing questions on what is wrong in the world and pointing to certain elements. Slowly things become clear, and then the media started covering the same topics which Q referred to. See the following:

- **End of ISIS**: think when Obama said this would go on, how did it finish. What is the connection to Benghazi or John McCain's photo with ISIS leader?

- **Saudi Arabia:** The Saudi Government coup where MBS took over as crown Prince changed many things. The purge in the Kingdom of Saudi Arabia brought in a change in laws in KSA. Q mentioned about KSA been one of three pillars holding the global cabal. Many secrets could have been known about the cabal with the detention of over 300 princes, ministers, and businessmen. This is, again, an inference.

Do search details about Prince Al-Waleed bin Talal, and his twitter spat with candidate Trump in 2015. Can there be no coincidences?

- **North Korea**: Why this regime (as called by media) at peace now. Trump and Kim meet multiple times? Harmony is almost close here.

- **Jeffery Epstein** – When the news of his arrest broke, there was a video after the press briefing. A reporter said that the Q folks will be jumping (why? Because they knew the story months before). This means the press is following the story, which Q already broke. Q mentions a lot of sexual assault and human trafficking. But do think about the following
    - NXIVM cult case: Organized sexual slavery carried out by certain celebrities backed by billionaire
    - Weinstein: Predator in Hollywood present. Many knew. But they choose to keep quiet.

  And now Jeffery Epstein. What you see is news

- **D5**: This has not come true, and I believe it is Decentralized Finance. DiFi. This will help liquidity and usher in a new wave of finance benefiting the people more than the bankers.

Nothing surprises me now in the world. So many stories the mainstream media places turn out to be fake or manipulated. And it is seen across the globe. You have seen this in the 4th estate vs. 5th estate chapter, and here were Q comes in. Cryptic posts are sent for people to find the truth. Look at the following post. It is long but read a few lines (the entire post is in the Appendix):

A person(s) value:
1. vote
2. monetary value (tax contribution)
3.
Why is 'free thought' ridiculed, challenged, and threatened when a person is opposed to the 'mainstream-narrative'?
[2] remains fixed (degree allowable by 'economic recession/expansion')
[1] remains a variable
[1] dependent on a 'controlled' system of information dissemination
What happens when 90% of the media is controlled/owned by (6) corporations?
What happens when those same corporations are operated and controlled by a political ideology?
What happens when the news is no longer free from bias?
What happens when the news is no longer reliable and independent?
What happens when the news is no longer trustworthy?
What happens when the news simply becomes an extension/arm of a political party?
Fact becomes fiction?

Fiction becomes fact?
When does news become propaganda?
Identity creation?
How does the average person, who is under constant financial stress (by design), find time to research and discern fact v fiction?
Majority of people more prone to believe someone in power sitting behind a big brand 'news' name?
Do people [human psyche] tend to follow the 'majority/mainstream viewpoint' in fear of being isolated and/or shunned?

Why do 'mainstream' media heads, within different orgs, always use the same keywords and/or catch phrases?
Coordinated? By who? Outside entity providing instructions?
Do they count on the fact that people [human psyche] are more prone to believe something if heard over-and-over again by different 'trusted' sources?
Do 'echo chamber' tactics provide validation / credibility to the topic/point being discussed?
Threat to intellectual freedom?
When you control the levers of news dissemination, you control the narrative.
Control of the narrative = power
When you are blind, what do you see?
They want you divided.
Divided by religion.
Divided by race.
Divided by sex.
Divided by political affiliation.
Divided by class.
When you are divided, and angry, and controlled, you target those 'different' from you, not those responsible [controllers].
Divided you are weak.
Divided you pose no threat to their control.
When 'non-dogmatic' information becomes FREE & TRANSPARENT it becomes a threat to those who attempt to control the narrative and/or stable [livestock kept – sheep].
When you are awake, you stand on the outside of the stable ('group-think' collective), and have 'free thought'.
"Free thought" is a philosophical viewpoint which holds that positions regarding truth should be formed on the basis of logic, reason, and empiricism, rather than authority, tradition, revelation, or dogma.
THIS REPRESENTS A CLEAR AND PRESENT DANGER TO THE CONSTITUTIONAL REPUBLIC OF THE UNITED STATES OF AMERICA.
Q

Do you remember the prayer at the start of the book? It was a Q drop. Why would a cult share a prayer and speak all religions needs to be respected as humans need to be respected? Why have Q posts and followers been attacked? Because the phenomena of Q have spread throughout the planet. When I looked at Google trends to see the details, the results did not surprise me anymore. See the top two images are the trends since the first post. And the bottom two are those in the last three months. It is spreading, and questions have been asked by the fifth estate.

Conclusion: This is why we need to question if Q is a LARP (Live action role-players) and a mere conspiracy theory like the JFK assassination, UFO, etc., then why to attack it this way. Why take down twitter accounts, YouTube channels. See the content that has been said. If Q or Q+ posts talked about violence, then the mainstream would have shown it or made a billboard about it. Be warned, fellow patriots and citizens of earth. The corporate media has an agenda. They are propaganda channels aimed to keep us asleep and not wake up. When the general population starts to question and demands an answer civilly, the Deep State does not want. They have control as long as we are divided. When we look at each other, what do you see? A fellow human soul with a heartbeat. Someone with feeling and life. Our unity and care for each other is our strength. The real question to ask is to see so many hit pieces are on it. Moreover, many media from print, broadcast, and virtual channels have come up news around the Q. Let's revisit the features again:

Questions based on Definition	Window of Perspective
Is It Far Right?	Can it be Far Right if it calls for equality, prayers, and calls for helping each other in posts? What it can be is that it is anti-globalization
Does it resemble a **Conspiracy Theory?**	Conspiracy theory or conspiracy fact. Q spoke about the Russian collusion as a Hoax. It is now seeming Q was right. See the release of documents valid. There are more such examples mentioned earlier
Does Cabal Exist?	Yes, Cabal does exist. Check out the SAFARI cabal where intelligence officers of certain countries with different interests worked together for particular agendas. And check the news of FVEY Intel collaboration. Such collaboration sometimes turns into Cabal.
Can Satan be worshipped	There is a Satan church in public views. Certain celebrities have shown signs of support
Are people (some politicians & celebrities) Pedophiles?	Do check for yourself. Just check Jeffery Epstein's story. A BBC report said that 5% of men are a pedophile. But search these terms Jimmy Savile, Bush Call Boy scandal to start with
Why does Child Trafficking exist?	Yes, it does. An example is already shared, and more are there. Even recently FBI arrested traffickers

Does this mean Q is always right? Does Q make mistakes? Maybe. A few posts were wrong or errors there – and the message used to come "on the move." A tweet shared a picture of a wide shot of a city from the sky showing the destruction. The tweet was saying one of the liberal channels was showing this. This picture was, in fact, from World War Z (I think). So, if military operation when, how such an error happened? Or was it deliberate to show that it is an ordinary person doing it and later the whole Q operation can be denied? I do not know.

When I think of the Q movement now, I am surprised to see what has happened over the last few weeks. The President was asked the question around QAnon. There was a Q drop months ago saying that the Question will be asked by the media. So, the question was asked in August 2020. This is what the President responded:

"Well, I haven't heard that, but is that supposed to be a bad thing or a good thing? You know, if I can help save the world from some problems, I'm willing to do it, I'm willing to put myself out there, And we are actually, we're saving the world from a radical left philosophy that will destroy this country, and when this country is gone the rest of the world would follow."

He did not deny it. Or accept it, but it was a way to bring more light. I also remember when Prime Minister of India Modi visited the US, he said few words when President Trump was on stage, which made me think, is this a COM (Communication) to Annons. PM Modi said, "President Trump has already done a lot for the world." The body language of POTUS changed for few seconds. He was sort of do not share more. Well, maybe I am reading a lot. I may be wrong, as I said before. But I would like to optimistic about the human race. What we need in this world is an open mind. A mind that can challenge and question everything. Q says to question and think for oneself.

As you can see from a couple of posts, it speaks about wanting to divide us. By race, color, religion, thought, etc. Imagine a world there is no war, and we will move forward together. The world produces enough food to feed everybody. Enough homes can be built so that no one needs to sleep without a roof on the head. And family values with love and care spread around.

Do you remember the Congress act on QAnon, which I wrote at the beginning of the chapter? Well, there is 17 number associated with it. Republicans who opposed it 17. Hmmm… 17 the number again. The final count of 18, 17 + 1. Q | Q+. Time will tell. And google trends do show the interest is increasing. Let's see what trends are shown for the Presidential Elections 2016 and what it shows in 2020.

Q: *V for Vendetta or Q for Queen (Chess)*

Q Clearance is a security classification equivalent to a United States Department of Defense Top Secret clearance. Just like in V for Vendetta (by Alan Moore), the protagonist fights a corrupt police state. His reason for his vendetta is because of the government that subjugated him. Q for the Queen is who moves to protect the King (commoner), and once in action, changes the game. Q is Justice and Q for QUAD?

CHAPTER 14
Google Trends | Great Awakening

After the midterm elections, the incumbent party holds more seats in the U.S. House of Representatives than after the previous midterm elections.

There are several unprecedented events amidst which the 2020 US Presidential elections are taking place. That makes it more challenging than ever before to predict the outcome of these elections. A pandemic that severely affected millions of Americans' health and lives, a struggling economy, recession, and a heap load of social issues that have certainly affected people's psychology are some of these factors. These are unprecedented times in history. And President Trump is going whatever he can in handling this situation. The nation needs confidence, and I believe this is what President Trump is showing as his aura. He is the one who can get the United States out of this vortex of crisis.

Computational Politics and Cyberspace Campaigning:
In this new era, the term "computational politics" has become more relevant than ever. Cyberspace has become the main battleground in which different presidential campaigns convey their messages to potential voters to convince them. Therefore, it is no surprise that previous records of campaign expenditure on advertisements are shattered each year. According to an estimate by Forbes in 2019, the election campaign this year has already seen an increase of 59% from the previous elections of 2016. The amount was estimated to be around 6.3 Billion US dollars. About 21% of political ads are placed on digital media, whereas on cable TV, 14% and only 5% are placed on the radio. These ratios highlight the application of digital marketing for political gains.

An interesting outcome of digital political campaigning and cyberspace as a political battleground is that people's political interests can be tracked online. The particular names, phrases, and the frequency they are searched in the United States of America and worldwide can predict the elections' outcome.

Its real-time and real-life collection of data pertaining to the political interests of people around the globe. While these predictions are 100%

accurate, it cannot be said that US presidential elections are notoriously difficult to predict. Many a time, the results deviate entirely from what the political analysts and experts have predicted. These data collections can indicate the public mood.

In light of this, can we say that one of the world's most widely used search engines, Google, can help us predict the next president? In an article published on modern democracy in April this year, Bhaso Ndzneze attempted to get an insight by analyzing Google Trends of the past. He wanted to see what they are suggestive of. He generated charts of popularity with the data obtained from Google Trends. Google searches for presidential candidates, incumbents, and eventual winners to have an interesting relationship. The scores were given so that a 100 indicated the most populous search, as a fraction of total searches, and 50 was the half of that or half as popular. Below are those generated charts. Let us see for a different period. The pattern is the same. Those who trended more won.

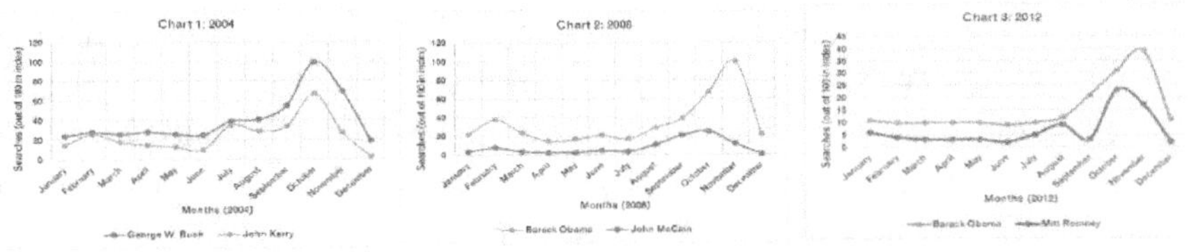

2016 Presidential Elections

What do google trends say about the elections? First, I wanted to check what is told in 2016. So, I looked at 3 months period – July 2nd, 2016, to October 2^{nd,} 2016.

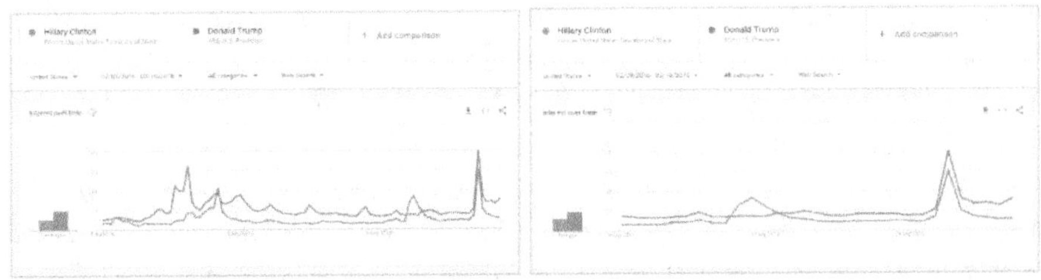

So, you can see Trump as a strong trend than Hillary. He was 1.5 higher than Hillary in the short term. When I check the data keeping the last 2 months before election day, Trump's gap was having numbers twice higher than Hillary. In the previous month, Trump was 42 at an interest level compared to 19 points of Hillary. The Red bar chart scored above blue. We know the result. He won the elections. Now let us see the same for the last 3 months for Trump vs. Biden. The date of the search is Oct 2nd.

2020 Presidential Elections

Coming to the 2020 elections, here are the trends.

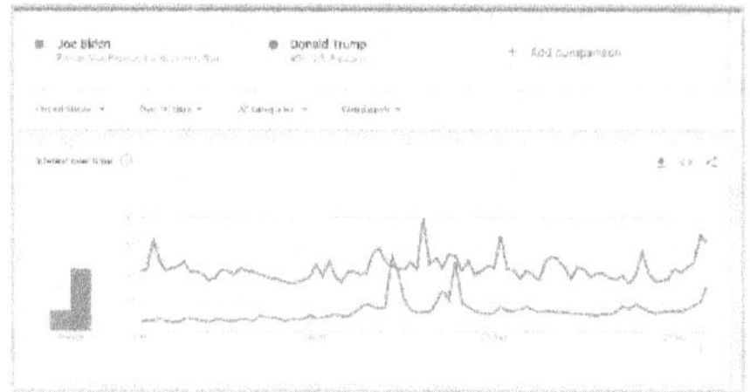 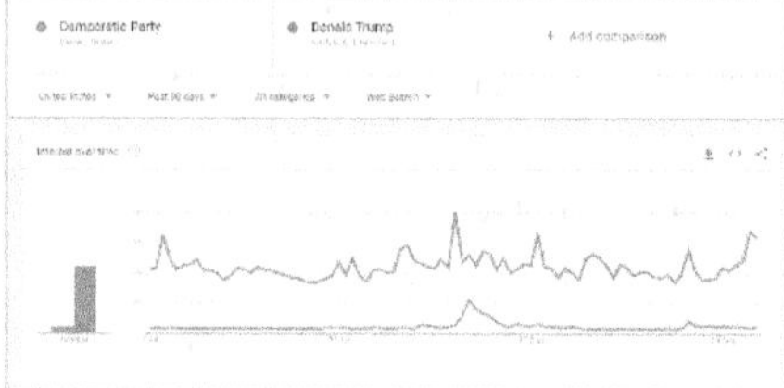

As you can see from the bar graphs, Trump scores both over Biden and the Democratic Party. The current ratio is 55 to 17. This is more than 3 times than of Joe Biden. This is higher than what Hillary had. Now when I check for one more before, it is 22: 64 in favor of Trump. This is again 3 times higher. Compared to where Donald Trump is scoring in interest, we compare it with Hillary in the 2016 period. And this is after the pandemic got it.

Great Awakening: *History reference, Colonial America*

In American colonial history, the Great Awakening was a religious revival in Christian evangelical activities. But it also led to the formation of the seeds of revolution and, ultimately, independence. In the 1740s and 1750s, a religious phenomenon swept the colonies from North to South. New ministers refused to convert to the Church of England and the preached (Q posts) in a New Light sort of way. This led to the Great Awakening. As new preachers spoke, America became less divided. There were new schools and churches. The Old Light Ministers did not like it and refused to follow the original form of preaching done by the New Light. More people came into the fold across different churches. Earlier ministers were elite and represented the upper class almost. The new faith was democratic, as their message was on equality (as understood then) and talked to break the differences.

CHAPTER 15
Predicting 2020 | Trust the Plan

After the midterm elections, the incumbent party holds more seats in the U.S. House of Representatives than after the previous midterm elections.

What if there was no Pandemic, and the world continued as it is, who would have you voted for? What would have been the election result? Donald Trump would have won a landslide. He can still win (he needs to win). Here I will share some publicly declared maps.

Trumps Path to Victory – the closest win scenario

Trump's win in the 2016 US presidential election is a story filled with thrill and sensation. It is attributed mainly to his capture of the battleground states. However, the story this year is a little different. President Donald Trump's campaign officials claim to win the election even without the blue wall states. These include the states of Pennsylvania, Michigan, and Wisconsin.

They claim that President Donald Trump will have a sure victory in Florida according to the electoral votes. He will also win in North Carolina. Along with these two, if he manages to hold all the states that he had earned a victory in, in the 2016 elections, then it would not matter if he does not get Pennsylvania, Michigan, Wisconsin, and even Minnesota. To retain his seat at the white house, Trump only needs to win one of these. However, Biden will have to win all four. As we have seen earlier, Hispanics will vote in large numbers, and it will help win Florida and Texas. In such a scenario, it will be advantageous to win Pennsylvania, it is by no means necessary.

Ryan Teague Beckwith, Reporter at Bloomberg, tweeted on September 29, regarding the pathways that can take Trump to victory. In the map, he pointed out that if Trump gains victory in the states of Arizona, Florida, North Carolina, and Maine's Second Congressional District, practically the states he had won in 2016, and adds Minnesota, He will have a pathway to victory even if he loses Wisconsin, Michigan, and Pennsylvania. In this scenario, the end result will be Trump 270 and

Biden 268. A narrow win and a slim chance but an entirely possible pathway.

The worse scenario would be a tie, with both candidates getting 270 mean Electoral College Tie. This can have disastrous consequences for the country (and the world).

There are other optimistic

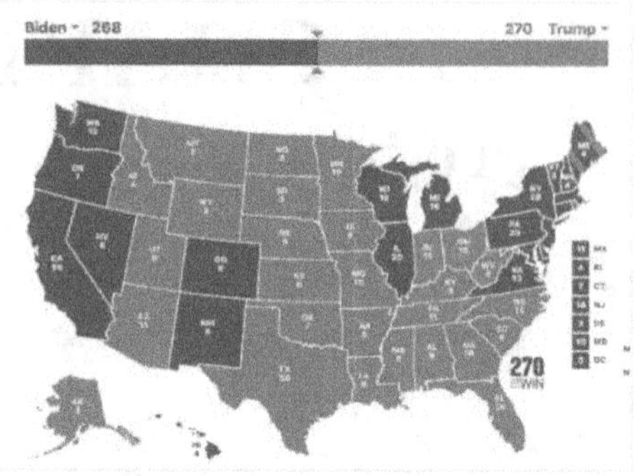

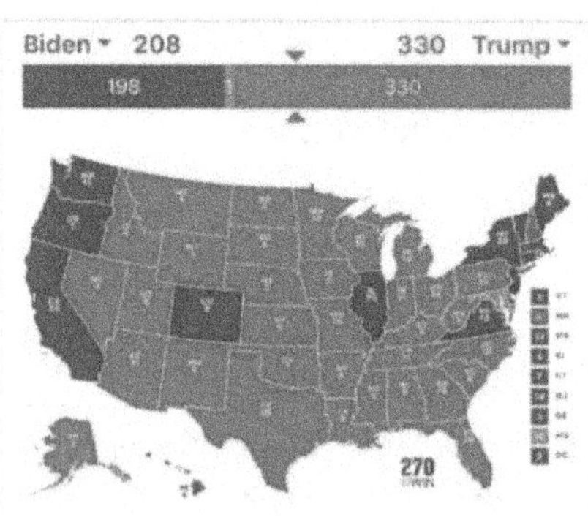

outlooks also. The first one was given by Kevin McCullough from @KMCRadio. He has proposed a 330 win to Trump. He has shared accurate(almost) calls in the last two elections.

The best model is the Primary Model by Helmut Norpoth. His model is the same one that I discussed in the earlier chapter. This model gives Trump 362 electoral votes and Biden 176. But what if there is no Biden as he has to step down, and another candidate has to come and take this place? Harris, Obama, Oprah, NY Gov, CA Govt?

Well, it can still be an electoral college victory. What is needed is a massive popular vote victory. Without such a triumph, the tensions will be high, and the results will still be questioned. Am betting on the following:

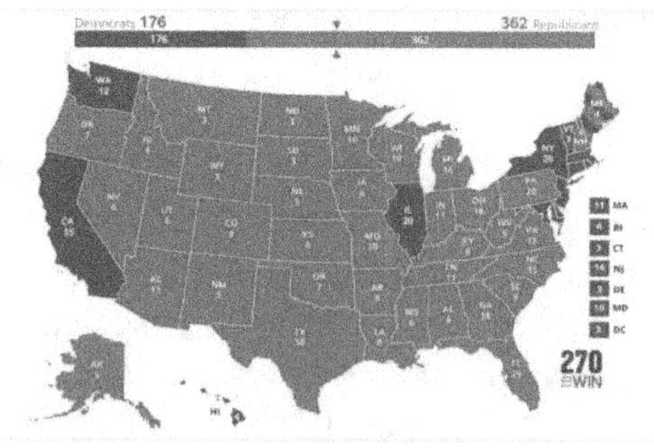

- Doubling African American votes from 6% to 12-15% (or 20%) with black male voters at 20% and females in high single digits.

- Rise in Hispanics across the board. Hispanic Catholics who voted in large numbers for Hillary will vote in higher numbers to Trump this period. It may be close to 35% (almost double from 2016)

- White voters who did not vote for Trump as they did not consider him a Republican candidate in 2016 will change their preference. Their votes will provide a boost to the popular vote
- The highest participation will be seen in various counties (rural and suburbs) this year. Their choice will be President Trump
- Due to no lack of a strong 3rd party candidate, a state like New Mexico will go towards Trump as more Hispanic votes will go for him
- Remember Utah, Senator Cruz won big in the Primaries, and Trump got less than 20%. Then in the Presidential elections, a 3rd party candidate got over 240,000 votes. There are more votes will move towards Trump (rise in the popular vote)
- In the age group of 30-49, there will be an increase in preference for Donald Trump. From 40%, it will be closer to 50%

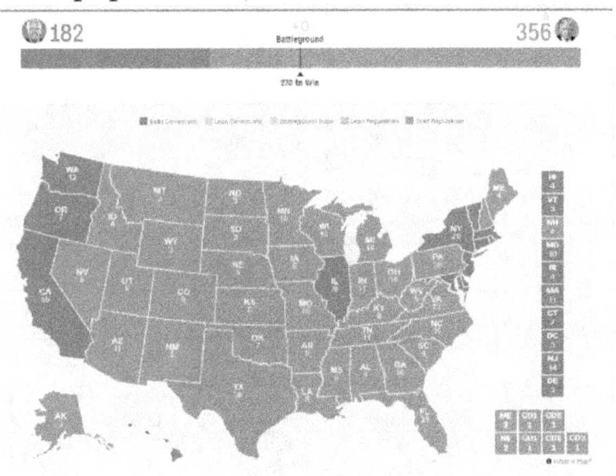

- Similar College grad voters will show a marginal increase for Trump from 36% to 38%-40%.

Based on these assumptions, President Trump could have won up to 356 if there were no Pandemic. Now, it can be any scenario. But his popular vote will be higher than last time.

Trust the Plan: *School of Life Reference*

Trust is an important word for the animal kingdom. We are always are at war, and when we trust something (Law/Government/Family), we keep our defenses down. When Trust is not present, we are ready to fight or become slaves. We need to trust the system to work, but it can only work if we have lawmakers we can trust. If not, then we need a plan. It can be a plan which has been in development for decades or centuries to ensure the Great Awakening leads to a future where there is less pain.

CHAPTER 16
If I am Wrong? | Future Proves Past

Buckle up, folks. History is being written. Something for future generations to read and understand. First, let's revisit the rating. It is 9 keys for me, and Trump wins. What about you?

Q	Factor	Question	Lichtman	Clark	You
1	Party Mandate	The incumbent's party gained House seats between midterm elections	FALSE	FALSE (?)	
2	Contest	There is no primary contest for the incumbent's party	**TRUE**	**TRUE**	
3	Incumbency	The incumbent is running for reelection	**TRUE**	**TRUE**	
4	Third-party	There is no third-party challenger	**TRUE**	**TRUE**	
5	Short-term economy	The short-term economy is strong	FALSE	FALSE	
6	Long-term economy	The long-term economic growth during the incumbent's term has been as good as the past two terms	FALSE	**TRUE**	
7	Policy change	The incumbent has made major changes to national policy	**TRUE**	**TRUE**	
8	Social unrest	There is no social unrest during the incumbent's term	FALSE	FALSE (?)	
9	Scandal	The incumbent is untainted by scandal	FALSE	FALSE (?)	
10	Foreign/ military failure	The incumbent has no major foreign or military failures abroad	**TRUE**	**TRUE**	
11	Foreign/ military success	The incumbent has a major foreign or military success abroad	FALSE	**TRUE**	
12	Incumbent (party) charisma	The incumbent is charismatic	FALSE	**TRUE**	
13	Challenger (party) charisma	The challenger is uncharismatic	**TRUE**	**TRUE**	
		Score	6 True	9 True	

I can totally wrong, and Trump loses big time. The Democrats will come to power, and history will be changed. In an alternate universe, Donald Trump may have won, and the world is saved. What future awaits only time will tell. The book is coming to an end, and I wanted to share a story. A personal story about when I visited the United States.

During one of my visits to the United States back around 2012, I was in Philadelphia doing touristy things. I went to a souvenir shop, trying to buy something to take back to India. When I started to check the items, it was all foreign-made. It was made in China, made in Vietnam, made in India, and more. I asked the shop assistant is there anything made in the United States, which I can buy. I still remember the blonde-haired teen eyes open wide. He said, "I don't think so, but we have something which is made in Mexico." I was like ok. I bought a T-Shirt. It was a Rocky one. The one in which it says, "His whole life was a million to one shot." (Something like President Trump now).

As I moved across stores, museums shop, I realized something wrong. It was ridiculously hard to find a "Made in America." Product. I walked to my tour bus, and then it dawned on me. I was on a tourist bus run by a Chinese – American company (assuming), having the tour guide (who was a student) and driver who had Chinese ethnicity. The bus was filled with Chinese tourists (from the mainland possibly). The bus was once taken to a specific store run by shopkeepers of Chinese ethnicity. It stored products with Made in China label. I was like thinking, United States of America was different from the one I visited in 1984 as a kid to Disneyland. Change is good. But if jobs go away, then social unrest can come. And this is where we need to find a balance in this globalized world. We need our media to be accountable. We need to able to believe what we see and hear and not be manipulated. No more misinformation, disinformation, and misinterpreted should be there. Somewhere I want to believe in the goodness of people. I want to believe in President Trump.

I hope he succeeds. From the point of view, the future of the planet depends on it. In time we will know. And maybe those reading this after the elections know the results. For me, this is the message I got from Project Looking Glass :). Don't ask me what this is. Think of it as individual observers with low latent inhibition can predict the future.

Future Proves Past: *Predictive Programming or Looking Glass*

An arrow, once fired, cannot go called back in the quiver. A prediction once shared remains. And the internet never forgets. I see the future as a play of probabilities and an ability to understand what will go wrong or right. Understanding nuances, like butterfly wings fluttering one, can see across the corner of reality.

CHAPTER 17+
Orange Man Not Bad

After the midterm elections, the incumbent party holds more seats in the U.S. House of Representatives than after the previous midterm elections.

Thank you for reading till now and for giving me a chance to me. I want to end my book with a few President Trump quotes, which defined and continue to represent his Presidency. And a few funny and satirical tweets. He has taken political correctness by the horns (am I allowed to write by the horns, or is it offensive to someone on this planet).

Quotes (Q+)

"Whether we are black or brown or white, we all bleed the same red blood of patriots."

Donald Trump, inauguration speech, 2017.

"The FAKE NEWS media ... is not my enemy; it is the enemy of the American People!"

February 7th, 2017

"Today, we finally acknowledge the obvious: that Jerusalem is Israel's capital,"

December 2017.

"We may have our differences, but we do well, in times like these, to remember that everyone who serves in our nation's capital is here because, above all, they love our country."

June 2017

"I can only hope that both Democrats and Republicans can come together for once for the good of the country." Donald Trump, on confirming Neil Gorsuch,

January 31st, 2019

"Terminated his evil reign of terror forever. Our message to the terrorists is clear: You will never escape American justice. If you attack our citizens, you forfeit your life!"

(General Soleimani death) January 3rd, 2020

"The next step forward in building an inclusive society is making sure that every young American gets a great education and the opportunity to achieve the American Dream. No parent should be forced to send their child to a failing government school." -

February 2020.

"One hundred and thirty-two lawmakers in this room have endorsed legislation to impose a socialist takeover of our health care system, wiping out the private health insurance plans of 180 million very happy Americans. To those watching at home tonight, I want you to know: We will never let socialism destroy American health care."

February 2020.

"My Admin has done more for the Black Community than any President since Abraham Lincoln. Passed Opportunity Zones with @SenatorTimScott guaranteed funding for HBCU's, School Choice, passed Criminal Justice Reform, lowest Black unemployment, poverty, and crime rates in history..." –

June 2nd, 2020.

"The people of this country are smarter than the people who cover them"

October 9, 2020

Tweets

Donald J. Trump
@realDonaldTrump
North Korean Leader Kim Jong Un just stated that the "Nuclear Button is on his desk at all times." Will someone from his depleted and food starved regime please inform him that I too have a Nuclear Button, but it is a much bigger & more powerful one than his, and my Button works!
6:49 PM · Jan 2, 2018
432.1K   291.8K people are Tweeting about this

Donald J. Trump
@realDonaldTrump
SANCTIONS
·ARE·
COMING
NOVEMBER 5
11:01 AM · Nov 2, 2018
173.8K   95.3K people are Tweeting about this

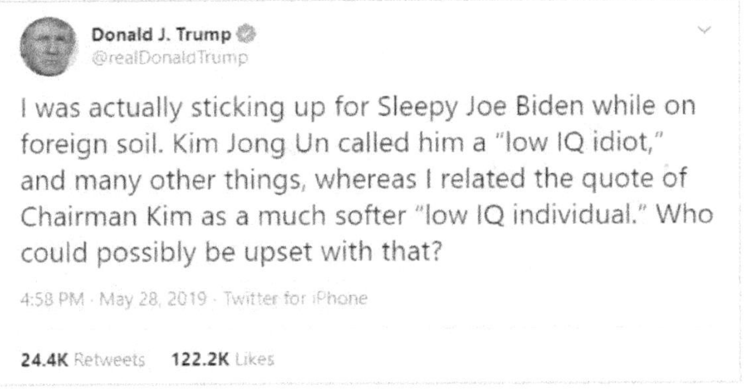

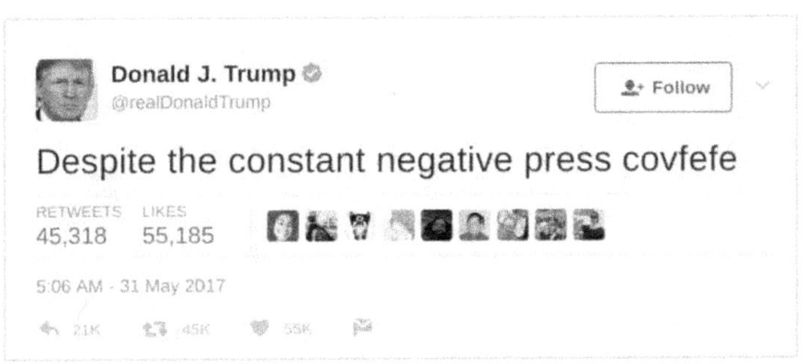

Yup, in the end, I expect the free thinkers to prevail. Freedom of diversity of thought is needed. None of us are perfect. But we still fight out fear. We fight for peace. I heard the following words once, "Si vis pacem, para bellum." This is Latin for "if we want peace, we need to prepare to war." This was we fight so we can go home to family. That is the way the human racc can move forward. President Trump has restored the idea of America. An America I am proud of. The shining light of Liberty, Justice, and Freedom. So, let's keep fighting and keep motivating each other. As in the end, Covfefe… we will prevail.

Appendix

Accomplishments of President Trump

What I tried here is to make a list of 123 achievements of President Trump. This was circulating in the virtual world, and mainstream media challenged this. There was fact-checking carried out by the NY times (I think), and though the Pandemic changed things, it still shows an honest attempt has made. The classification is the following:

- True (83): Verified, even by mainstream media
- True, but challenged (24): Was True till the pandemic, or there were other factors for success like bipartisan reasons
- True* (13): Was True till the pandemic, but once recovery happens, these points will change
- False (3): Either the situation changed due to Pandemic, or there may be other reasons for the point.

#	Accomplishments	Fact Check
1.	Trump passed three bills regarding Native Americans: funds for Native language, compensation for land loss for the Spokane tribe, and the Little Shell Tribe of Chippewa Indians in Montana	True (but challenged)
2.	Space force was finalized as the 6th form of Military.	True
3.	Trump passed a bill against animal cruelty with tougher punishments for offenders.	True
4.	There was an annual decrease in violent crime during the Trump administration.	True
5.	CBD and Hemp were made legal after the 2019 Farm Act for use in pharmaceuticals.	True
6.	To counter the water infrastructure problem in Flint, Michigan, $100 million in funds was awarded by Trump EPA.	True
7.	The USA became the largest producer of crude oil in 2018.	True
8.	Trump signed a law ending the gag order for pharmacists to ensure that drug prices remain transparent for the public.	True
9.	A bill against sex trafficking was passed that helped tackle the issue on a large scale.	True

10.	Friendly Airport Mothers Act of 2017 allowed special care areas for breastfeeding mothers in airports.		True
11.	The 25% of lowest-paid Americans enjoyed a 4.5% income boost in November 2019, which outpaces a 2.9% gain in earnings for the country's highest-paid workers.		True*
12.	The minimum wage limit was increased by Trump, and entry-level jobs paid higher.		True (but challenged)
13.	For wildlife protection and conservation, Trump allocated 375,000 acres of protected land.		True (but challenged)
14.	An ocean cleaning scheme under Save our Seas was selected to receive over $10 million in funding annually.		True
15.	A bill was passed to allow drugs to be imported from Canada for a more affordable market.		True
16.	Trump passed a bill forcing hospitals and health care centers to be transparent about their prices so that consumers can better understand insurance options.		True
17.	He mandated that transparent medical service charges on bills were necessary to provide the public with a clear understanding of their bills.		True
18.	Hospitals are required to post their standard charges, including the possible discount rates, for transparency in dealings.		True (but challenged)
19.	Under Trump's reign, drug prices are on a steady decline annually, compared to a steady increase before the Trump administration.		True (but challenged)
20.	The creation of the White House VA Hotline helped veterans voice their concerns across the country.		True
21.	The Department for Veteran affairs was thoroughly audited, with many employees fired or demoted over incompetence.		True
22.	An executive order was issued requiring better health plans for American veterans.		True
23.	A bill passed by Trump proposed a 3.1% increase in salaries of federal employees, the hight in the decade.		True (but challenged)
24.	Trump administration extended paid paternal leave for up to 12 weeks for federal employees.		True

25.	Free HIV drug provision to 200,000 uninsured patients annually for 11 years was announced by Trump.	True
26.	Record retail sales during the 2019 holiday season, over $729 billion.	True
27.	Trump allowed group insurances for small businesses for better affordability.	True (but challenged)
28.	President Trump signed the Preventing Maternal Deaths Act for better research and understanding of maternal complications in Black Americans.	True
29.	The First Steps act of 2018, signed by President Trump, improved the justice systems and helped inmates adjust to society.	True
30.	The First Steps Act addressed inequalities in the conviction system that harmed Black American discriminately.	True
31.	The First Step Act expanded judicial discretion in the sentencing of nonviolent crimes.	True
32.	Over 90% of those benefiting from the retroactive sentencing reductions in the First Step Act are Black Americans.	True
33.	The rehabilitation programs mandated by the First Step Act help inmates return easily to society and lead a new life.	True (but challenged)
34.	Trump increased funding for Historically Black Colleges and Universities (HBCUs) by more than 14%.	True (but challenged)
35.	Trump passed a bill forgiving the debt of Historically Black Colleges and Universities considering Hurricane Katrina.	True
36.	Compared to 2018, there has been a 31.6% increase in single-family home sales in 2019.	True
37.	HBCUs were prioritized when the executive director was moved to the White House from the Department of Education.	True
38.	Trump received the Bipartisan Justice Award at a historically black college for his criminal justice reform accomplishments.	True (but challenged)
39.	The poverty level fell to 11.6% during the Trump administration, a record after 17 years.	True

40.	For Hispanic-Americans and African Americans, poverty rates were the highest ever recorded.	True*
41.	Trump reauthorized the Land and Water, Conservation fund, expanded natural reserved land, and allotted wilderness protection areas of 1.3 million acres.	True (but challenged)
42.	Trump's U.S.D.A. committed $124 Million to rebuild rural water infrastructure.	True
43.	Consumer confidence & small business confidence is at an all-time high.	False
44.	Trump administration created more than 7 million jobs during the term.	True*
45.	More Americans are now employed than ever recorded before in our history.	True*
46.	More than 400,000 manufacturing jobs created since his election.	True*
47.	Trump appointed 5 openly gay ambassadors.	True
48.	Ric Grenell, a gay ambassador, appointed by Trump, is leading the fights against the criminalization of homosexuality globally.	True
49.	The anti-Trafficking Coordination Team (ACTeam) initiative by Trump helped the law enforcement double the convictions in the problem.	True (but challenged)
50.	In 2018, a leading online sex-trafficking advertisement organization was taken down by the Department of Justice.	True
51.	Trump's new guidelines regarding sex-trafficking cases have helped authorities combat the issue effectively.	True (but challenged)
52.	Around 1588, criminals associated with human trafficking were arrested under the Immigration and Customs Enforcement's Homeland Security Investigations.	True
53.	The National Human Trafficking Hotline was supported and given funds.	True
54.	The hotline identified 16,862 potential human trafficking cases.	True
55.	The Department of Justice financially supported organizations that help victims of human trafficking.	True*

56.	For human trafficking, more victim assistant specialists have been hired by the Department of Homeland Security.	True
57.	Trump asked for a bill on school choice legislation to allow children to move to a better school regardless of zip code.	True (but challenged)
58.	The President signed funding legislation in September 2018 that increased funding for school choice by $42 million.	True (but challenged)
59.	Trump passed tax cuts that will help families utilize 529 college savings plans for primary and secondary education of children.	True
60.	Under his leadership, ISIS has lost most of its territory and has been largely dismantled.	True
61.	ISIS leader Abu Bakr al-Baghdadi was killed.	True (but challenged)
62.	For the first time after 2006, the Perkins C.T.E. was reauthorized with over $1 billion in funds annually for educational and vocational programs to the states.	True
63.	Executive order expanding apprenticeship opportunities for students and workers.	True
64.	An executive order was issued that prohibited religious discrimination in the US government.	True
65.	Trump signed an executive order that allows the government to withhold money from college campuses deemed to be anti-Semitic and who fail to combat anti-Semitism.	True
66.	The administration stopped any funding to international organizations that may be involved in performing or funding abortion.	True
67.	Venezuela faced increased sanctions for socialists who are involved in the killing of citizens.	True
68.	A new trade deal was signed with South Korea.	True
69.	US energy exports to the European Union were increased according to the agreement.	True
70.	The Us government withdrew from the Trans-Pacific Partnership to create more American jobs.	True

71.	Secured $250 billion in new trade and investment deals in China and $12 billion in Vietnam.	True
72.	Up to $12 billion were proposed in compensations for unfair trade to farmers.	True
73.	Trump administration has freed over a dozen American hostages overseas.	True
74.	The Music Modernization Act was signed, with changes proposed to copyright law.	True
75.	Funding in billions of dollars was secured for the construction of a wall at the US-Mexico border.	True
76.	Rehabilitation for inmates includes second-chance jobs being offered to inmates to re-establish themselves.	True (but challenged)
77.	The 'Ready to Work Initiative' was introduced by the Department of Justice and the Board of Prisons to aid inmates in getting jobs after term.	True
78.	New tax cut laws were introduced to promote investment in low-income areas across the country, called the Opportunity Zone Incentives.	True
79.	8,764 Opportunity Zones have been labeled nationally.	True
80.	The Opportunity Zones are expected to generate $100 billion yearly in revenue in economically distressed areas.	True
81.	Trump directed the Education Secretary to end Common Core.	True (but challenged)
82.	The 9/11 Victims Compensation Fund was signed and accepted into law.	True
83.	Veterans suicide prevention programs were introduced.	True
84.	Due to the Tax Cut and Jobs Act of 2017, over a trillion dollars were brought back to the US from overseas.	True
85.	Manufacturing jobs were growing at the fastest rate since 30 years ago.	True (but challenged)
86.	The stock market has reached record highs.	True*
87.	The median household income is at a record high.	True

88.	Unemployment rates for African Americans are the lowest yet.		True*
89.	Unemployment rates for Hispanic Americans are the lowest yet.		True*
90.	Unemployment rates for Asian Americans are the lowest yet.		True*
91.	Unemployment rates for women are the lowest in 65 years.		True*
92.	Unemployment rates for the youth are the lowest in 50 years.		True*
93.	We have the lowest unemployment rate ever recorded.		False
94.	Job training in private corporations was boosted to 4 million people because of the Pledge to America's Workers act.		True
95.	95 percent of U.S. manufacturers are optimistic about the future — the highest ever.		True*
96.	Small businesses experience the lowest marginal tax rates in 80 years due to the Republican tax bill.		False
97.	A lot of existing regulations were removed in favor of new ones to help support small businesses.		True
98.	Able-bodied adults without dependents on welfare programs were taken off and required to look for work after the new Welfare reform.		True
99.	FDA approved more affordable drugs during the Trump administration that before.		True
100	New reforms on Medicare help low-income seniors save on drug costs, restricting hospitals from overcharging.		True
101	The Right-To-Try bill was passed, which allowed terminally ill patients to try alternative treatment methods that were previously not permitted.		True
102	To combat the opioid epidemic, over $6 billion were secured in funds.		True
103	The VA Choice Act and VA Accountability Act were signed, according to which telehealth services for veterans, as well as walk-in clinics and emergency services, were enhanced.		True
104	US Crude Oil production is at an all-time high, leading to less import from the Middle East.		True*

105	The USA became an exporter of natural gas for the first time since 1957.	True
106	Due to Trump's pressure campaigns and reforms, NATO allies had an increase in defense spending.	True
107	Withdrew the United States from the job-killing Paris Climate Accord in 2017, and that same year, the U.S. still led the world by having the largest reduction in carbon emissions.	True (but challenged)
108	Under the new administration, Trump's nominees for the circuit court judge are confirmed much faster than previous administrations.	True (but challenged)
109	Trump's nominees for the Supreme Court Justice, Neil Gorsuch, and Brett Kavanaugh were confirmed.	True
110	The US Embassy in Israel was moved to Jerusalem from Tel Aviv.	True.
111	New trade deals were signed with neighboring countries Mexico and Canada, sparking new job opportunities.	True
112	A new agreement was finalized with the European Union to increase American exports.	True
113	A Part One trade deal was sparked with China due to the country's previous unfair trading practices, intellectual property theft, and forced technological transfer, which resulted in increased tariffs.	True*
114	New legislation was signed to improve the National Suicide Hotline.	True (but challenged)
115	To improve research on childhood cancer and advance treatment, detailed and most comprehensive legislation regarding childhood cancer was passed.	True
116	According to the TCJA of 2017, child tax credit limits have almost double, and the bars for income limits of parents have been increased so more families can claim the benefits.	True
117	The Tax Cut and Jobs Act also created a new category for dependent credit that does include child credit.	True
118	Trump increased the funding for the Child Care and Development Act by $2.4 billion, making the total amount $8.1 billion to states for childcare programs.	True

119	The Child and Dependent Care Tax Credit (CDCTC) signed into law by Trump provides a tax credit equal to 20-35% of child care expenses, $3,000 per child & $6,000 per family + Flexible Spending Accounts (F.S.A.s) allow you to set aside up to $5,000 in pre-tax $ to use for child care.	True (but challenged)
120	The CARES Act was passed in 2019, which granted $1.8 billion in funds over five years to autism affected individuals and their families.	True
121	Trump allotted over $19 million to Lupus research and foundations, with $41.7 billion to the National Institutes of Health, summing up to a record funding for lupus research.	True
122	A new bill against telecommunication fraud called the Telephone Robocall Abuse Criminal Enforcement, and Deterrence (TRACED) is the first of its kind to act against telemarketing offenders.	True
123	The US stock market continues to hit record highs during the Trump administration.	True (but challenged)

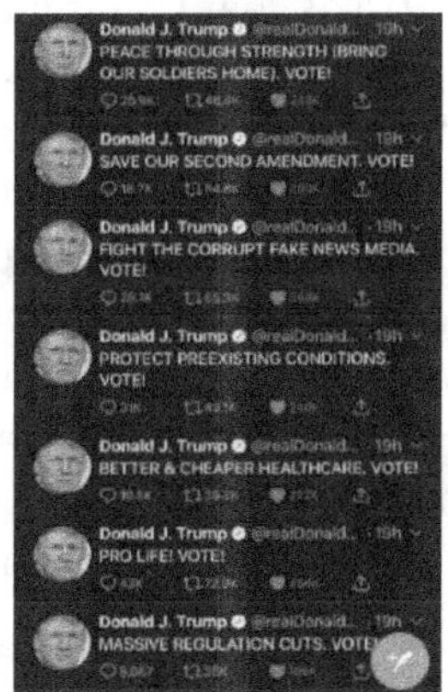

Q: Alternative Reality or Psyops

The more you know the Truth, there will be a Great Awakening. There will be Those Who Scream the Loudest as they have knowingly committed Crimes Against Humanity. They thought You Would Follow the Stars. The Mockingbird Fake News Media kept you sleeping. They are truly the Enemy of the People. They are Political Action Group.

You will hear Booms. But when the Storm is Upon US, the world will hear BOOM BOOM BOOM.

What you read above are some of the terms Q uses in his drops. From the various 5th estate and some 4th estate sources, the following is the hypothesis on what is Q and who is Q:

1. **What is Q?**
   The theory is that Q a military intelligence operation for information dissimilation to the public. The aim is to increase citizen awareness of what is happening in the world behind the curtains.

2. **What is Going behind the Curtains?**
   The hypothesis is that there is a global cabal (Deep State) who are/were in control of world affairs. This group has been active for many years (centuries according to some). Their objective to usher in One World Government with a control structure similar to communism (maybe a China-like model of social scoring).

3. **What would this mean?**
   This would mean the end of democracy, freedom, and liberty. There would be a new class structure, and billions of people are turned into serfs to serve the overlord.

4. **How can this be true?**
   Think why, after so many years, we are not able to solve problems. Is it human nature that we do not want to help each other? Or some powers want to keep people under debt, countries under servitude. Think why ISIS, a threat, got eliminated so soon. Why North Korea, which was supposed to be a rogue state, is trying to find peace. Read

about the FinCen files where Banks allowed trillions of dollars of dirty money to be moved by criminals and drug lords.

5. **Ok, this is something at the international level. How does it impact me? I am just in a county in the United States.**

There was an article in the Wall Street Journal and Politico in 2016, which talked about billionaire Soros funding local prosecutors. That period he gave at least $3.8 million to political-action committees backing candidates for district attorney. Why is this important for you as funding always comes with the agenda? And as more Left-Leaning (assuming he will be backing such) prosecutors win elections, then think if there can make a difference in policy opinions leading to change in arrest rules or not prosecuting further. See the Jussie Smollett case where he tried to create hatred between groups by a false accusation. The prosecutor dropped all charges, and he walked away (for now). Now the bigger picture. If these local prosecutors get involved in the post-election declaration of results, then what happens? A coup. Even Attorney General William Barr has warned about Soros, who is bankrolling radical prosecutor candidates in cities across the country to challenge the United States. As individual agendas will be driven actively. This is, again, Deep State activity.

Think the 2018 governor elections in Florida where the vote difference was less than 35,000 in a total of over 8 million votes. The Republic candidate won. Imagine if the other candidate Andrew Demese Gillum would have won, what would have happened? You do remember he was caught in an intoxicated state with meth and a gay escort. (Think J. Epstein now). But for 35,000 votes, things would have been different (for worse – think NY with Dem governor and the nursing home rules during pandemic times). But they tried. According to Gov. Rick Scott, Liberals (Democratic strongholds) counties in Broward and Palm Beach were trying to steal the election. The counting kept going and took more time than other counties (was this a dry run for 2020). Even the Courts sided with Gov.Scott and asked the county to release the voter information as votes came out nowhere. This is why election ID is required.

I know this has been a long answer. But it is needed to understand how the Deep State operates. In short, entrenched bureaucracy is supported by a funded political and legal system good for Freedom. Deep State operations are a challenge for Founding Fathers' vision.

6. **Do we know who Q is?**

It is not one single person. What is known is that it is a group of fewer than 10 persons who know complete operation.

7. **Where does Trump fit in this?**

Trump was asked to run for President by this group to save the United States as a country and the world to ensure continuity of liberty and freedom. There are some posts marked as Q+, which the digital warriors believed to be President Trump's call sign.

8. **How will this end?**

The expectation is that there will be a purge of these evildoers who have committed crimes of grievous nature – murder, rape, corruption, child trafficking, pedophilia, cannibalism, and more. They will be taken to the Guantanamo Bay detention camp, where Military Tribunal trials will be held. According to Q, the NSA (National Security Agency) has all pieces of evidence. It is assumed that the big pieces of evidence are in Anthony Weiner's laptop.

For those who forgot, Wiener was close to Hillary Clinton. He and his wife Huma Abedin (Vice-Chair of Hillary 2016 campaign) got married by President Bill Clinton. Their reception was in the Clinton home. He was sentenced to 21 months in prison as he sexted a 15-year minor child. On his laptop, there was Hillary's missing email of the private email server. This case got reopened in Oct-2016 by the FBI. But they did not release all info and did not prosecute Hillary. This chapter can be reopened soon. Hope Truth and Justice prevails.

9. **Can Q be a psyop and Donald Trump a boogeyman?**

It can be. All this can be an elaborate psyop by Deep State assets in the US, China, Russia, the CIA, etc. Psyop is a psychological operation that aims to release selective information to a UI (Useful Idiot) and audiences to influence their emotions and take away their objective reasoning ability. If this is the case, it can be for winning the election only or worse and install the one-world government's deep-state plan without the citizens fighting back. It can be a psyop aimed at that part of the population that can fight back. This way, they are identified and later rounded up.

Now am I being too alarmist in saying this. Think of all communist and fascist movements in history. It has led to the death of millions and the detention of thousands who opposed it. Some examples:

- Bolshevik revolution (Russia) led by Lenin in Russia
- Culture revolution (China) led by Mao Zedong
- Khmer Rouge (Cambodia) led by Pol Pot

If you ask me what will happen? I can only say, keep walking. Trust the Plan but VERIFY. Keep the mind open to search for information and notice signs of disinformation or misinformation. Connect with your family and loved ones. Keep healthy habits and And keep Questioning. One such question around the Deep State I had asked in a literary festival in Delhi, India. I was laughed at by the crowd and retired bureaucracy, which was part of the panel. They never heard of Deep State, they said. I just shrugged it off. I posted about this interaction on twitter and forgot about it.

You can see the screenshot on the right. What I did not realize that my twitter post had been Qed. Yes, Q posted my post around the question bout the deep state. Screenshots below. He

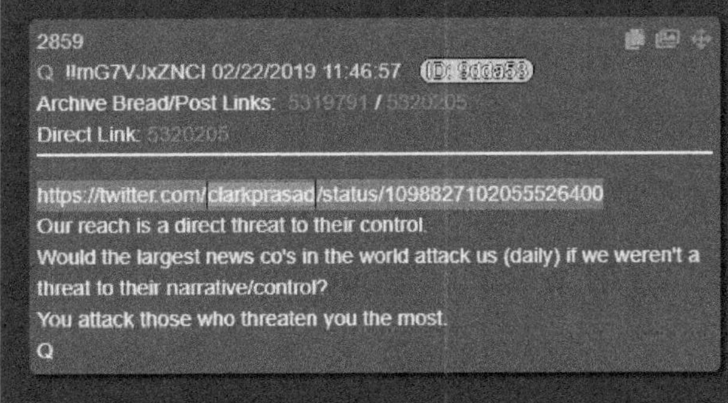

spoke about the attack from the mockingbird fake news media, which have become propaganda arms. His words, "Our Reach is a direct threat to their control. Would the largest news co's in the word attack us (daily) if we weren't a threat to their narrative/control? You attack those who threaten you the most. Q.

So, you see how there is a coordinated attack on taking down QAnons FB pages, twitter accounts, YouTube channels, and many media coverage around how and why Qanon is terrible and wrong. The question I have is, can the media take a Q post where they speak of violence or harm. Many of the posts have links available in the public domain, and what is said, we need to do our own research. The media's fear is the failure to hold narrative control over the various sheep around the planet.

Below are screenshots of google trends in four countries: India, Switzerland, Japan, and Brazil. The word searched in the trend, QAnon, in three years. You can clearly see a pattern. People are questioning the narrative or trying to investigate the truth if Q is LARP or a conspiracy.

Sample Q Posts

Post

"We hold these truths to be self-evident, that all men are created equal, that they are endowed by their Creator with certain unalienable Rights, that among these are Life, Liberty and the pursuit of Happiness. —That to secure these rights, Governments are instituted among Men, deriving their just powers from the consent of the governed, —That whenever any Form of Government becomes destructive of these ends, it is the Right of the People to alter or to abolish it, and to institute new Government, laying its foundation on such principles and organizing its powers in such form, as to them shall seem most likely to effect their Safety and Happiness. Prudence, indeed, will dictate that Governments long established should not be changed for light and transient causes; and accordingly all experience hath shewn, that mankind are more disposed to suffer, while evils are sufferable, than to right themselves by abolishing the forms to which they are accustomed. But when a long train of abuses and usurpations, pursuing invariably the same Object evinces a design to reduce them under absolute Despotism, it is their right, it is their duty, to throw off such Government, and to provide new Guards for their future security."
– Declaration of Independence
We Will Do Our Job to Protect the Vote.
Will You Do Yours?
Will You Answer the Call?
WWG1WGA!!!
Q

Post

A person(s) value:
1. vote
2. monetary value (tax contribution)
3.
Why is 'free thought' ridiculed, challenged, and threatened when a person is opposed to the 'mainstream-narrative'?
[2] remains fixed (degree allowable by 'economic recession/expansion')
[1] remains a variable
[1] dependent on a 'controlled' system of information dissemination
What happens when 90% of the media is controlled/owned by (6) corporations?
What happens when those same corporations are operated and controlled by a political ideology?
What happens when the news is no longer free from bias?
What happens when the news is no longer reliable and independent?
What happens when the news is no longer trustworthy?
What happens when the news simply becomes an extension/arm of a political party?
Fact becomes fiction?
Fiction becomes fact?
When does news become propaganda?
Identity creation?

How does the average person, who is under constant financial stress (by design), find time to research and discern fact v fiction?

Majority of people more prone to believe someone in power sitting behind a big brand 'news' name?

Do people [human psyche] tend to follow the 'majority/mainstream viewpoint' in fear of being isolated and/or shunned?

'Mainstream' is used for a reason [dominate trend in opinion].

[If majority of people believe 'x' then 'x' must be validated / true]

Why do 'mainstream' media heads, within different orgs, always use the same keywords and/or catch phrases?

Coordinated? By who? Outside entity providing instructions?

Do they count on the fact that people [human psyche] are more prone to believe something if heard over-and-over again by different 'trusted' sources?

Do 'echo chamber' tactics provide validation / credibility to the topic/point being discussed?

Threat to intellectual freedom?

Would control over[of] these institutions/organizations allow for the mass control of a populations viewpoint re: a desired topic?

Read again – digest.

Would control over[of] these institutions/organizations allow for the mass control of a populations viewpoint re: a desired topic?

THINK BLM PUSH EVERY 4-YEARS.

Logical thinking.

Why, after the election of 2016, did [D]'s and media corps jumpstart a [coordinated & planned] divisive blitz intended to create falsehoods re: illegitimacy of election, character assassination of POTUS through sexism, racism, every other 'ism'?

How much of the population still believes POTUS colluded w/ RUSSIA due to MSDNC 365-blitz?

No MSDNC retraction of POTUS_RUSSIA collusion narrative [propaganda]? _why?

Pre/post 2016 election?

Why were[are] violent [masked] terror orgs such as Antifa immediately created/funded and allowed to operate within [D] controlled cities [safe-zones]?

Why were these orgs tasked w/ immediate intimidation/shut down of any pro-POTUS rally[s] and/or events?

Why were marches immediately organized to counter and silence pro-POTUS rally[s] and/or events?

Why were marches immediately organized which divided people into sex/gender, race, [ism]?

When you control the levers of news dissemination, you control the narrative.

Control of the narrative = power

When you are blind, what do you see?

They want you divided.

Divided by religion.

Divided by race.

Divided by sex.

Divided by political affiliation.

Divided by class.

When you are divided, and angry, and controlled, you target those 'different' from you, not those responsible [controllers].

Divided you are weak.

Divided you pose no threat to their control.
When 'non-dogmatic' information becomes FREE & TRANSPARENT it becomes a threat to those who attempt to control the narrative and/or stable [livestock kept – sheep].
When you are awake, you stand on the outside of the stable ('group-think' collective), and have 'free thought'.
"Free thought" is a philosophical viewpoint which holds that positions regarding truth should be formed based on logic, reason, and empiricism, rather than authority, tradition, revelation, or dogma.
THIS REPRESENTS A CLEAR AND PRESENT DANGER TO THE CONSTITUTIONAL REPUBLIC OF THE UNITED STATES OF AMERICA.
Q

To see how Q has given news far ahead of time:
https://www.qproofs.com/

There can still be doubts if Q is real or not. The mockingbird media has been covering news around the topics which Q hinted. The media mocks on the idea of child pornography. But there more and more news coming around this hideous crime. In Sep 2019, more than 600 law enforcement personnel were involved in the anti-cybercrime operation in Germany. This operation shut down an old underground NATO bunker, which had fence and surveillance cameras. What was happening in this bunker? The operators provided Bulletproof hosting – which means IT infrastructure that protects online criminal activity from government intervention. 200 servers were seized, among many things. The servers were established in 2013.

Now imagine, so much could have been done over the years – the purchase of servers, the movement to the bunker in a sleepy riverside town, and no one questioned. Why? Are each one of us really a sheep, and we will do and believe whatever narrative is given to us. Humans have evolved over hundreds and thousands of years to now aiming to create planetary colonies and thinking of interstellar travel. We need to keep our logical and inquisitive mind active. Even if Q is not really, the questions he is forcing us to ask are real. Why cannot the world be at peace? Why can we not ensure no one sleeps hungry? Why we cannot trust each other and not be divided. Fellow citizens of the world. Rise up. Rise higher and help each other. May God bless America and the entire planet. This is our time. Our moment. Our history we are creating. Faith is important. Family is important. Good over evil. From Darkness to Light, we need to go. For now, let us Trust the Plan. But help each other in times of crisis. Thank you. And Namaste from India, Planet Earth.

The END... or a start to a new beginning?

A Note to Planetary COVID Warriors

To all the Physicians, Nurses, Pharmacists, Healthcare Professionals, Law Enforcement officers, Sanitation Workers, Janitors, and numerous other professionals, a BIG, Thank You from our souls. All of you frontline warriors are like fighting for humanity from the trenches. You and your family deserve every nation's respect. In the end, we all are humans. And humanity is defined by compassion and care for our fellow brethren. There are already stories written about you. The future generation will always remember you. Thank You once again.

A Note to Earth's Digital Warriors

Let us keep asking questions. Let's us keep the discourse going. Let us keep an open mind and challenge the status quo. There is a lot of doubts about what will happen soon. But remember your loved ones and take care of your families. Thank You to those who helped me bring this together. Thanks IPOT, B2T, RP76, Praying Medic, JoeM and many others.
WWG1WGA.

REFERENCES

Chapter 1:
https://finance.yahoo.com/news/birth-big-data-simulmatics-predicted-131505357.html

Chapter 2:
https://www.nature.com/articles/d41586-020-02607-8
https://finance.yahoo.com/news/birth-big-data-simulmatics-predicted-131505357.html
https://www.sas.upenn.edu/~baron/journal/18/18124/jdm18124.html
http://primarymodel.com/
https://www.huffpost.com/entry/trump-nearcertain-to-defe_b_9403762?1457390306=
https://www.researchgate.net/publication/24116339_Predicting_Elections_from_Politic
ians'_Faces
https://repository.upenn.edu/cgi/viewcontent.cgi?article=1156&context=marketing_pa
pers
https://www.brookings.edu/articles/forecasting-the-presidential-election-what-can-we-
learn-from-the-models/
https://repository.upenn.edu/cgi/viewcontent.cgi?article=1157&context=marketing_pa
pers
https://blogs.lse.ac.uk/usappblog/2016/04/15/our-biographical-model-predicts-clinton-
would-defeat-trump-by-a-landslide-but-would-be-tied-with-cruz/
https://repository.upenn.edu/cgi/viewcontent.cgi?article=1156&context=marketing_pa
pers

Chapter 3:
Kollanyi, B. et al (2016)
Social Bots Distort the 2016 U.S. Presidential Election Online Discussion. First
Monday, Vol. 21, No 11
https://link.springer.com/article/10.1057/s41270-016-0010-2
https://theconversation.com/how-did-we-get-the-result-of-the-us-election-so-wrong-
68566
https://www.nationalgeographic.com/news/2016/11/presidential-election-predictions-
history/

Chapter 4:
https://www.washingtonpost.com/news/the-fix/wp/2016/09/23/trump-is-headed-for-a-
win-says-professor-whos-predicted-30-years-of-presidential-outcomes-correctly/
https://bethesdamagazine.com/bethesda-magazine/march-april-2017/how-bethesdas-
allan-lichtman-predicted-the-election-for-trump/
https://www.businessinsider.com/obama-cant-lose-allan-lichtman-is-never-wrong-
except-this-time-2011-9?IR=T
https://www.npr.org/sections/itsallpolitics/2012/11/09/164711093/what-earthquakes-
can-teach-us-about-elections?sc=ipad&f=1003
https://www.schwartzreport.net/what-earthquakes-can-teach-us-about-elections/
https://www.ctvnews.ca/world/america-votes/after-predicting-trump-s-2016-win-allan-
lichtman-says-he-knows-who-s-going-to-win-in-2020-1.5081463
https://www.imediaethics.org/did-professor-allan-lichtman-correctly-predict-the-
winner-of-the-2016-presidential-election-his-own-book-says-no/
https://www.nytimes.com/2020/08/05/opinion/2020-election-prediction-allan-
lichtman.html#commentsContainer

https://www.nytimes.com/2020/08/05/opinion/2020-election-prediction-allan-lichtman.html#commentsContainer
https://www.imediaethics.org/did-professor-allan-lichtman-correctly-predict-the-winner-of-the-2016-presidential-election-his-own-book-says-no/
https://pollyvote.com/en/components/models/mixed/keys-to-the-white-house/
https://www.imediaethics.org/did-professor-allan-lichtman-correctly-predict-the-winner-of-the-2016-presidential-election-his-own-book-says-no/
https://www.investopedia.com/terms/h/heuristics.asp
https://en.wikipedia.org/wiki/Heuristic
https://repository.upenn.edu/cgi/viewcontent.cgi?article=1157&context=marketing_papers
https://www.washingtonpost.com/news/the-fix/wp/2016/09/23/trump-is-headed-for-a-win-says-professor-whos-predicted-30-years-of-presidential-outcomes-correctly/
https://www.american.edu/media/news/092616-13-keys-prediction.cfm

Chapter 5:

https://www.brookings.edu/wp-content/uploads/2016/06/Vital-Statistics-Chapter-2-Congressional-Elections.pdf
https://www.bbc.com/news/election-us-2016-37889032
http://legendsrevealed.com/entertainment/2016/10/21/did-dick-gregory-accidentally-receive-over-nine-million-votes-in-the-1968-presidential-election/
https://en.wikipedia.org/wiki/1968_United_States_presidential_election
http://archive.fairvote.org/plurality/perot.htm
https://www.theguardian.com/us-news/ng-interactive/2016/nov/08/us-election-2016-results-live-clinton-trump?view=map&type=presidential
https://www.oberlo.in/blog/small-business-statistics#:~:text=1.-,How%20Many%20Small%20Businesses%20Are%20There%20in%20the%20U.S%3F,has%20fewer%20than%20500%20employees.
https://fingfx.thomsonreuters.com/gfx/rngs/USA-ECONOMY-TRUMP/01008133219/index.html
https://www.statista.com/statistics/270001/distribution-of-gross-domestic-product-gdp-across-economic-sectors-in-the-us/#:~:text=This%20statistic%20shows%20the%20distribution,percent%20from%20the%20service%20sector.
https://www.bea.gov/data/gdp/gdp-industry
https://www.cia.gov/library/publications/resources/the-world-factbook/fields/214.html
https://en.wikipedia.org/wiki/List_of_countries_by_GDP_sector_composition
https://www.whitehouse.gov/briefings-statements/historic-results-president-donald-j-trumps-economic-agenda/
https://www.businessinsider.in/slideshows/miscellaneous/trump-boasts-the-economy-is-the-best-its-ever-been-here-are-9-charts-showing-how-its-fared-compared-to-the-obama-and-bush-presidencies-/slidelist/71525978.cms#slideid=71525984
https://fred.stlouisfed.org/series/MEHOINUSA672N
https://www.whitehouse.gov/briefings-statements/historic-results-president-donald-j-trumps-economic-agenda/
https://ourworldindata.org/grapher/average-real-gdp-per-capita-across-countries-and-regions?time=2008..2016&country=~USA
https://www.thebalance.com/real-gdp-per-capita-how-to-calculate-data-since-1946-3306028#:~:text=Real%20GDP%20per%20capita%20is,people%20and%20adjusted

%20for%20inflation.&text=The%20first%20concept%20is%20%E2%80%9Cgross,co
untry%20produces%20in%20a%20year.
https://corporatefinanceinstitute.com/resources/knowledge/economics/stimulus-check/
https://www.economist.com/graphic-detail/2020/09/02/how-did-americans-use-their-
coronavirus-stimulus-cheques
https://voxeu.org/article/how-us-consumers-use-their-stimulus-payments
https://www.nber.org/papers/w27693
https://www.texaspolicy.com/trumps-economy-keeps-humming-manufacturing-
adding-more-jobs-than-government-reversing-obama-trend/
https://thehill.com/opinion/campaign/479579-trumps-big-reelection-weapon-a-
remarkable-manufacturing-jobs-boom
https://www.epi.org/publication/reshoring-manufacturing-jobs/
https://fred.stlouisfed.org/series/MEHOINUSA672N
https://www.federalregister.gov/presidential-documents/executive-orders/donald-
trump/2020
https://en.wikipedia.org/wiki/List_of_executive_actions_by_Donald_Trump
https://www.heritage.org/markets-and-finance/commentary/middle-class-incomes-
surging-thanks-trump-policies
https://www.theguardian.com/business/2020/feb/27/small-business-owners-donald-
trump-second-term
https://www.surveymonkey.com/curiosity/cnbc-small-business-q1-2020/
https://www.oberlo.in/blog/small-business-statistics#:~:text=1.-
,How%20Many%20Small%20Businesses%20Are%20There%20in%20the%20U.S%3
F,has%20fewer%20than%20500%20employees.
https://www.surveymonkey.com/curiosity/cnbc-small-business-q2-2017/
https://www.surveymonkey.com/curiosity/cnbc-small-business-q2-2018/
https://www.surveymonkey.com/curiosity/cnbc-small-business-q2-2019/
https://www.washingtonpost.com/news/the-fix/wp/2016/09/23/trump-is-headed-for-a-
win-says-professor-whos-predicted-30-years-of-presidential-outcomes-correctly/
https://bethesdamagazine.com/bethesda-magazine/march-april-2017/how-bethesdas-
allan-lichtman-predicted-the-election-for-trump/
https://en.wikipedia.org/wiki/Shooting_of_David_Dorn
https://ucr.fbi.gov/crime-in-the-u.s/2017/crime-in-the-u.s.-2017/tables/table-8/table-
8.xls/view
https://en.wikipedia.org/wiki/Aloys_P._Kaufmann#:~:text=Kaufmann%20was%20electe
d%20to%20his,the%20voters%20in%20April%201944.
https://en.wikipedia.org/wiki/Louis_Miriani#:~:text=Miriani%20(January%201%2C%20
1897%20%E2%80%93,to%20serve%20as%20Detroit's%20mayor.
https://en.wikipedia.org/wiki/List_of_mayors_of_Cleveland
https://en.wikipedia.org/wiki/List_of_mayors_of_Milwaukee
https://en.wikipedia.org/wiki/List_of_mayors_of_Kansas_City,_Missouri
https://www.ncbi.nlm.nih.gov/pmc/articles/PMC3485346/
https://www.huffpost.com/entry/charisma-learn-the-secret_b_9234862
https://www.pewresearch.org/fact-tank/2019/05/15/facts-about-us-political-
independents/

Chapter 6:

https://www.270towin.com/

http://crystalball.centerforpolitics.org/crystalball/2020-president/
https://cookpolitical.com/analysis/national/national-politics/new-survey-results-kffcook-political-report-survey-az-fl-and-nc
https://cookpolitical.com/sites/default/files/2020-09/EC%20Ratings.091720.3.pdf?
http://insideelections.com/ratings/president
https://www.270towin.com/2020-election-forecast-predictions/
https://www.voanews.com/2020-usa-votes/who-will-win-2020
https://www.brookings.edu/articles/forecasting-the-presidential-election-what-can-we-learn-from-the-models/
https://www.epi.org/publication/swa-wages-2019/#:~:text=Between%202018%20and%202019%2C%20the,%2Dpercentile%20wage%20grew%202.0%25

Chapter 7:

Bhutel, B. (2020, Sep 20) "October Surprise' might be more surprising this time," Asia Times. Retrieved 24 September 2020, from https://asiatimes.com/2020/09/october-surprise-might-be-more-surprising-this-time/
Chaggaris, S. (2020, Sep 21) "Analysis: US election 'October surprise' comes early," Al Jazeera. Retrieved September 23, 2020, from https://www.aljazeera.com/news/2020/9/21/analysis-us-election-october-surprise-comes-early
Gee, T. (2020, July 16). 15 October Surprises That Wreaked Havoc on Politics. Politico Magazine. Retrieved September 24, 2020, from http://www.bbc.com/news
October surprise: Does it ever swing a US election? (2016, October 30). Retrieved September 24, 2020, from http://www.bbc.com/news

Chapter 8

https://hbcudigest.com/obama-vs-trump-who-did-more-for-hbcus-through-their-first-two-years/
Bureau, U. (2019, May 23). Moves to and From the South and West Dominate Recent Migration Flows. Retrieved September 30, 2020, from https://www.census.gov/library/stories/2019/04/moves-from-south-west-dominate-recent-migration-flows.html
Bureau, U. (2020, August 17). "Median Household Income, Poverty Rates, and Computer and Internet Use." Retrieved September 30, 2020, from https://www.census.gov/newsroom/press-releases/2018/2013-2017-acs-5year.html
Frey, W. (2019, January 31). How migration of millennials and seniors has shifted since the Great Recession. Retrieved September 30, 2020, from https://www.brookings.edu/research/how-migration-of-millennials-and-seniors-has-shifted-since-the-great-recession/
Thompson, D. (2019, September 17). American Migration Patterns Should Terrify the GOP. Retrieved September 30, 2020, from https://www.theatlantic.com/ideas/archive/2019/09/american-migration-patterns-should-terrify-gop/598153/

Source:
https://www.pewresearch.org/politics/2018/08/09/an-examination-of-the-2016-electorate-based-on-validated-voters/
https://edition.cnn.com/election/2018/exit-polls
https://edition.cnn.com/election/2016/results/exit-polls
https://www.pewresearch.org/fact-tank/2020/08/20/key-findings-about-u-s-immigrants/
https://www.y-axis.com/news/where-do-migrants-to-us-come-from/
https://www.migrationpolicy.org/article/immigrant-veterans-united-states-2018
Thompson, Simon (December 3, 2010). "Voting Rights: Earned or Entitled?". Harvard Political Review.
Levy-Uydeda, Ray (March 3, 2020). "Why some U.S. citizens won't get to vote for president because of where they live"
https://www.americanimmigrationcouncil.org/research/immigrants-in-the-united-states
https://oiac.org/iranian-community-usa/
https://www.pewresearch.org/fact-tank/2020/03/02/how-border-apprehensions-ice-arrests-and-deportations-have-changed-under-trump/
 https://www.brennancenter.org/our-work/research-reports/what-first-step-act-and-whats-happening-it
https://www.baltimoresun.com/business/bs-bz-opportunity-zones-20190730-3b3koim5wfcovhnp6t32ja2h4m-story.html
https://www.whitehouse.gov/briefings-statements/president-donald-j-trump-delivering-promise-empower-lift-nations-forgotten-communities/
https://www.sentencingproject.org/publications/one-year-after-the-first-step-act/
Puente, M (2020, Sept. 25) "Nearly One Third Of Latinos Vote Republican, But Who Are The Trump Supporters?", WBEZ, Retrieved 2nd October 2020 from,
https://www.wbez.org/stories/nearly-one-third-of-latinos-vote-republican-but-who-are-the-trump-supporters/90cc2448-a7e5-4b2f-8e34-d26e1a681318
Torregrosa, L (2020, Sep 16) " Latino voter support that's as strong as ever. Why haven't his insults cost him?", Nbcnews. Retrieved 2nd October 2020 from
https://www.nbcnews.com/think/opinion/trump-has-latino-voter-support-s-strong-ever-why-haven-ncna1240168
Ordonez, F. (2020, September 24) "With Warnings Of Socialism, Trump Seeks To Boost Support Among Young Florida Latinos" NPR, Retrieved 2nd October 2020 from
https://www.npr.org/2020/09/24/916067522/with-warnings-of-socialism-trump-seeks-o-boost-support-among-young-florida-lati
https://www.statista.com/statistics/191694/number-of-law-enforcement-officers-in-the-us/#:~:text=In%202019%2C%20there%20were%20697%2C195,in%202013%20with%20626%2C942%20officers.

Chapter 9

https://www.nytimes.com/2020/09/23/opinion/latino-voters-trump.html
https://www.washingtonpost.com/politics/2020/09/29/power-up-trump-campaign-lowers-expectation-three-states-he-flipped-2016/
https://twitter.com/ryanbeckwith/status/1310896264901537792
https://projects.fivethirtyeight.com/2020-election-forecast/
https://www.census.gov/quickfacts/fact/table/US/RHI725219

https://fee.org/articles/everything-you-need-to-know-about-blue-state-fiscal-problems-in-one-chart/
https://www.city-journal.org/democrat-states-midterms
https://edition.cnn.com/2020/10/07/politics/electoral-college-joe-biden-donald-trump/index.html

Chapter 10

Payne, Gregory(1986). Tom Bradley
Elder, Janet. (May 16, 2007). "Will There Be an 'Obama Effect?'", The New York Times
Black, Chris. (November 9, 1989). "POLLSTERS SAY SOME VOTERS LIE,," Boston Globe
https://en.wikipedia.org/wiki/Bradley_effect#cite_ref-22
https://www.dailykos.com/stories/2016/8/28/1563638/-Trump-campaign-hopes-for-reverse-Bradley-Effect
Brenan, M. (September 26th, 2019). Americans' Trust in Mass Media Edges Down to 41%. *Gallup Organization.* Retrieved from
https://news.gallup.com/poll/267047/americans-trust-mass-media-edges-down.aspx
Hayden, E. (September 20th, 2010). Obama: 'Fox News' Point of View is 'Destructive'. *The Atlantic.* Retrieved from
https://www.theatlantic.com/politics/archive/2010/09/obama-fox-news-point-of-view-is-destructive/339970/
Investors' Business Daily. (October 10th, 2018). Media Trump Hatred Shows In 92% Negative Coverage Of His Presidency: Study. Retrieved from
https://www.investors.com/politics/editorials/media-trump-hatred-coverage/
Swift, A. (April 5th, 2017). Six in 10 in U.S. See Partisan Bias in News Media. *Gallup.* Retrieved from https://news.gallup.com/poll/207794/six-partisan-bias-news-media.aspx

Chapter 11

The Editors of Encyclopaedia Britannica. (2018, Nov 20) "Fifth column", Encyclopædia Britannica, inc. Retrieved Sep 28, 2020 from https://www.britannica.com/topic/fifth-column
Churchill, W. (June 4, 1940). "We Shall Fight on the Beaches". winstonchurchill.org. Retrieved July 25, 2017.
Pedrick, C. (1990, Nov 14) "CIA organized Secret Army in Western Europe." Retrieved Sep 28, 2020 from
https://www.washingtonpost.com/archive/politics/1990/11/14/cia-organized-secret-army-in-western-europe/e0305101-97b9-4494-bc18-d89f42497d85/
Clark, C. (2020) "Deconstructing Deep States", Government Executive, Retrieved Sep 28, 2020 from https://www.govexec.com/feature/gov-exec-deconstructing-deep-state/

Chapter 12

Goldberg, Michelle (August 17, 2020). "Opinion | Trump Might Cheat. Activists Are Getting Ready". The New York Times. ISSN 0362-4331. Retrieved August 24, 2020.
Nwanevu, O. (2020, Sep 14) "The Ridiculous War-gaming of the 2020 Elections", The Soap Box. Retrieved 28 Sep 2020, from
https://newrepublic.com/article/159352/wargaming-2020-election-trump-biden
Preventing a Disrupted Presidential Election and Transition, Report by TIP (2020, August 3) Retrieved 28 Sep,2020, from
https://assets.documentcloud.org/documents/7013152/Preventing-a-Disrupted-Presidential-Election-and.pdf
Sirohi, S. (2020, Sep 14) "A period of uncertainty could follow this US election," Observer Research Foundation. Retrieved 28 Sep 2020, from
https://www.orfonline.org/expert-speak/a-period-of-uncertainty-could-follow-this-us-election/
Solender, A. (2020, Jul 19) "Trump Refuses To Commit To Accepting Election Results," Forbes. Retrieved 28 Sep, 2020, from
https://www.forbes.com/sites/andrewsolender/2020/07/19/trump-refuses-to-commit-to-accepting-election-results/#3da328cc5add

Chapter 13

https://economictimes.indiatimes.com/news/international/world-news/all-about-qanon-the-pro-donald-trump-conspiracy-theory-that-is-going-viral-as-us-polls-near/articleshow/77625603.cms
https://historycollection.com/10-historic-presidential-scandals/10/

Chapter 14

source:https://moderndiplomacy.eu/2020/04/02/can-these-6-worldwide-google-search-trends-predict-the-2020-us-presidential-election/
https://www.ushistory.org/us/7b.asp

Chapter 15

https://twitter.com/ryanbeckwith/status/1310896264901537792
https://twitter.com/KMCRadio/status/1313319927542091777
https://edition.cnn.com/election/2020/electoral-college-interactive-maps

Chapter 16

https://en.wikipedia.org/wiki/Transition_Integrity_Project
https://www.wbur.org/onpoint/2020/07/28/election-war-games-trump-scenario
https://paxsims.wordpress.com/2020/08/04/transition-integrity-project-preventing-a-disrupted-presidential-election-and-transition/
https://newrepublic.com/article/159352/wargaming-2020-election-trump-biden
https://news.harvard.edu/gazette/story/2020/08/stealing-an-election/
https://www.usatoday.com/story/news/politics/elections/2020/08/06/election-2020-war-games-trump-vs-biden-race-show-risk-chaos/5526553002/
https://www.orfonline.org/expert-speak/a-period-of-uncertainty-could-follow-this-us-election/

https://www.express.co.uk/news/world/1333117/Donald-Trump-election-2020-us-riot-violence-latest-Joe-Biden-US-president-vote
https://nationalinterest.org/blog/reboot/how-2020-election-could-be-close-and-disputed-1876-168777
https://www.vox.com/policy-and-politics/2020/8/18/21371964/2020-transition-integrity-project-simulation-trump
https://www.thetrumpet.com/blogs/61-andrew-miiller/22906-democrats-quietly-preparing-for-post-election-violence

Chapter 17

https://www.buzzfeednews.com/article/ellievhall/qanon-trump-rally-conspiracy-theory
https://slate.com/technology/2020/09/qanon-identity-revealed-explained.html
https://abcnews.go.com/Politics/men-qanon/story?id=73046374
https://www.theweek.co.uk/95197/who-is-q-and-what-is-qanon
https://www.bbc.com/news/53498434
https://www.dnaindia.com/ahmedabad/report-mumbai-human-trafficking-case-turns-into-one-of-human-smuggling-2652539
https://ahmedabadmirror.indiatimes.com/ahmedabad/crime/mumbai-police-nab-kingpin-of-racket-involved-in-trafficking-children-to-us-in-gujarat/articleshow/65424097.cms
https://www.firstpost.com/india/kingpin-involved-in-trafficking-300-children-to-us-arrested-in-gujarat-charged-rs-45-lakh-for-each-4977611.html
https://www.congress.gov/bill/116th-congress/house-resolution/1154/text
https://www.euronews.com/2017/01/20/key-quotes-from-donald-trump-s-inauguration-speech
https://twitter.com/realDonaldTrump/status/832708293516632065
https://www1.cbn.com/cbnnews/israel/2017/december/president-trumps-full-statement-on-jerusalem-we-finally-acknowledge-the-obvious-that-jerusalem-is-israels-capital
https://www.newyorker.com/news/john-cassidy/donald-trump-flashed-a-presidential-sideand-then-went-back-to-ranting
https://twitter.com/realDonaldTrump/status/890196164313833472?ref_src=twsrc%5Etfw
https://www.washingtonpost.com/graphics/2018/opinions/the-year-in-trump-quotes/
https://www.nbcnews.com/politics/donald-trump/trump-soleimani-strike-his-reign-terror-over-n1110226
https://reason.com/2020/02/04/trump-school-choice-state-of-the-union-opportunity/
https://usaherald.com/opinion-trumps-2020-state-union-address-best-history/
https://twitter.com/realDonaldTrump/status/1267885675338219520

Appendix:

https://www.wsj.com/articles/billionaire-soros-funds-local-prosecutor-races-1478194109
https://www.politico.com/story/2016/08/george-soros-criminal-justice-reform-227519
https://www.newsbreak.com/news/1478038997012/ag-barr-soros-funded-dem-prosecutor-candidates-will-lead-to-increased-crime-fewer-police-officers
https://www.bbc.com/news/uk-54226107
https://www.npr.org/2020/08/17/903368305/investigation-finds-abuses-and-failures-in-handling-of-first-jussie-smollett-cas
https://www.bbc.com/news/world-us-canada-51469713
https://nypost.com/2020/03/14/man-busted-with-andrew-gillum-in-hotel-room-with-meth-was-gay-escort/
https://www.denverpost.com/2018/11/09/florida-election-controversy/
https://time.com/5450501/florida-recount-2018/
https://www.politico.com/news/magazine/2020/09/16/governor-ron-desantis-florida-trump-410244
https://www.daytondailynews.com/news/national/who-anthony-weiner/mdWtaa2yGHBmUlsvZWFGIO/
https://www.insider.com/lone-fbi-agent-reopened-hillary-clinton-investigation-2019-10
https://thewire.in/world/darknet-cybercrime-servers-hosted-in-former-nato-bunker-in-germany
https://www.dw.com/en/darknet-cybercrime-servers-hosted-in-former-nato-bunker-in-germany/a-50618469

About Suraj Clark Prasad

Suraj Clark Prasad, alter ego of Suraj Prasad, could be called a mixed citizen. Born in a leap year (year of Rocky, All the President's Men, Omen) in Lagos, Nigeria, he lived most of his life in New Delhi. He had his education in Lagos, Delhi, Mangalore, and Kozhikode.

A pharmacist (from Mangalore University, NGSMIPS) with a management degree from IIM Kozhikode, Baramulla Bomber was his first book. He has written a sci-fi short story titled Mirror-Mirror. His first education on the mysteries of the universe came via Carl Sagan's *Cosmos*. Since then, he has never looked back on reading, watching, and discussing the universe. During the Cold War days, he grew up with BBC radio was one of his mysterious companions as a kid, when his father played the news regularly every day. World War II news and documentaries on CIA- KGB tussle kept him engaged. As a kid, he wanted to be an archaeologist or an astronaut. Still, fate had its own road, and he got involved with Mr. Carbon, aka Chemistry. Currently, he is a healthcare management consultant.

Besides writing, traveling, and hiking, he is involved in alumni-related activities for his Alma Mater.

Clark's favorite authors are Robin Cook, Jeffery Archer, Robert Ludlum, Frederick Forsyth, and Tom Clancy. Books like *The Odessa File*, *Patriot Games*, *Coma*, *Not a Penny More, Not a Penny Less*, and of course *Da-Vinci Code* are some of his favorites. He is based at Bengaluru, Planet Earth, Milky Way Galaxy.

Website: www.clarkprasadk.com
Twitter: @clarkprasad

Facebook:
https://www.facebook.com/Clark-Prasad-The-Official-Fanpage-188104207902785/

9 798696 408873